The Gi... ...

Pompey

Conversations with the Dead!

Bryony Best

ISBNs:
Paperback: 978-1-80227-611-4
eBook: 978-1-80227-612-1

Cover design by Publishing Push
Cover photo by Stuart Best
www.bryonybest.com

A Thank You from the Author

I would like to dedicate this book to all the lost souls out there. For anyone who has been trapped in a dark tunnel with no ray of hope, may this book be your shovel ....

To Mother – *"I am only a warrior because of the life I have lived, and that life started within you."*

To my fiancé – *"Thank you for your unconditional love."*

To my best friend Sadie – *"I love you with all my heart; you are my person."*

To my unofficial agent Emma – *"Thank you for always believing in me."*

To my red-haired, fire demon friend – *"Your help and support has been immeasurable."*

To my neighbour Lucie – *"You truly are a selfless person, thank you."*

To my dearest family and friends – *"Without your support and love, I wouldn't be me."*

To my dear friend and teacher – *"Paul, you taught me well and I thank you."*

To the Portsmouth Temple of Spiritualism – *"Without your guidance and the safety of your establishment, I would certainly be elsewhere."*

To all the team at Publishing Push – *"Thank you for believing in my story before all the others did."*

Bryony Best

XOXOXO

Contents

Introduction

I can hear screaming and ringing in my ears. Where am I?

It sounds like I am underwater, with muffled voices and noises that I cannot quite work out. I can smell something strange, like blueberries.

I open my eyes, searching for answers or something that looks familiar. I look ahead, and I can see cars facing me. Why are they facing me?

FUCK .... I'm on the motorway!

The date was December 11th at 4.12 pm, and the year is 2021. My blue Citroen car is facing the wrong way on the A27 motorway, and I, my friend, am well and truly fucked.

For me to share this experience with you, an experience that I am naming Crash Test Dummy the 2nd, I will need to take you back to May 15th, 2021, where it all began ...

My name is Bryony Best, and I am just another ordinary human. I am an ordinary human who has survived some extraordinary circumstances. Many people like to tell me that I am lucky; I do not feel this way. I feel like I am a survivor who has been forced into many unwanted or undeserved situations, like a fly that has wriggled free from a predator's web of lace and lies.

I have cheated death on numerous occasions; the Grim Reaper himself fears going toe to toe with me. He can chew on my bones, and he will choke on my spleen before he vomits me back to this earth plane. It is not my time to leave; my time is far from now.

How do I know that it is not my time to travel up to the great spirit in the sky?

I am glad you ask. The same way that I knew that my life would be full of both beautiful and horrific experiences. I have always been different to my siblings; my father used to give me this look ...

Let's go back to the start. Journey with me to 1984.........

Chapter 1

"Oh my God, she is coming; the baby is nearly here. You are doing great, Daffney, one more big push …"

The lights are flickering in St Mary's Hospital in Portsmouth, and it is a cold and wet day which is typical for January. Michael is reading his crossword, hoping to finish it before the baby is born. It is nearly three o'clock in the afternoon, and he is already bored of this labour.

It is a baby girl; the nurse has to clean her up as she is covered in shit. That is how Bryony entered the world: pure and innocent but covered in shit.

People say witnessing a birth of a baby is a miracle; well, they haven't paid attention to the poor woman ripping her body in half. The mother-to-be endures horrible pain and labour just to release the parasite that has been suckling all her nutrients for 40 weeks. With a newborn baby in her arms and both blood and shit on the bed from the ordeal, a miracle has passed. Once the baby screams and you look into their curious eyes, all is forgotten, and all is forgiven, for a new life has been released into this world. It is a miracle.

The baby is new, helpless, and absolutely breathtaking.

My memories as a small child were of my family living in a busy and tidy household as my mother ran a tight ship. My father would often play his guitar, and we all lined up to sing songs. My dad's family are from Ireland and are all very talented musically. My father was a legend, he had played in a band and sung at many talent shows and, quite often, he won. When my dad would sing the song Unchained Melody and hit all the high notes, well, the crowd would go wild. In Ireland, there is a place called the Guildhall, and we have a Guildhall here in Portsmouth too. My father would be hired to sing on stage, and the place would be packed to the brim with punters wanting to hear him sing.

My dad was a Catholic, and my mother a Spiritualist, so my mother did not discuss her beliefs with my father. As a child, I would often be naughty or play up; being the youngest of seven and living with two older brothers wasn't always easy.

My dad would cup my face with his hands, look deep into my eyes and say, "I can see the devil; he is dancing in your eyes, now tell me what happened."

I would be faced with two options: to confess my sins and be spared the punishment or to lie and risk his wrath. More often than not, I would confess. Let's face it; no one wants the leather belt.

It is now, as an adult, that I understand my dad was less conventional than most. I can pass an innocent comment or remark, only to be faced with horrified looks and gasps of shock from others. I will give you an example: I once said at work that my dad used to suffocate us from behind while whispering, "This will make you stronger." As I sat there laughing alone, the room fell silent, and my co-workers stared at me like I was a teabag in a coffee shop.

My best friend and the love of my life is Mercedes, she always has my back, and we soon created a system to avoid my over-sharing or "over-scaring," as I used to call it. If I am to say something that is ordinary to me, but that is extraordinary to others, she will quiet time me. The system worked a treat and was flawless until we changed jobs, and Mercedes was no longer there to quiet time me when it was needed.

As a child, maybe aged three, I recall lying in bed and squeezing my eyes shut. When I opened my eyes to take a look, I would see shapes and colours, shadows and objects. I believed that this is what all people saw, but I would soon discover there was more to this than meets the eye.

Like many children, I admit I had my fair few accidents of wetting the bed. This was not because I would urinate during my sleep; it was for fear of running into the dark to the bathroom. My family lived in a three-bedroom council house with a large back garden, and a noisy but comforting pigeon shed. From the pavement, the front garden was small, with grass on the left side and a concrete area for a car on the right. The main front door had a concrete overhang, and a side door was located to the left of the garden. Living in Portchester was a very special time for me, way better than when we moved to less desirable Paulsgrove. As you entered the front door, you could turn left into the kitchen, and inside the kitchen were two doors. One door led to the dining room and front room, and the other led to a long utility hall with a toilet. The stairs were a right turn to the bedrooms; bedroom one was smelly and large as it was my two older brothers, Brand and Arren's, room. The next door along was my bedroom, which would soon have a broken black and white television with an aerial as it was the eighties! We only required a three bed-house as my older siblings had grown up, and moved out. My parent's bedroom and a bathroom were at the end of the landing.

As children, we would share a bath, yes, all three of us in the bath! The tiles around the bathroom displayed scratch and sniff stickers from the dentist, the only kid-orientated evidence that children lived in the house. I fought with my siblings, as all kids do. We rarely played, but when we did, it was like average children. I marched behind Brand in the garden, pretending we were soldiers with my father's work helmets on our heads and large sticks as our guns. My father raced pigeons, a popular hobby in the eighties. We had two sheds in the garden: a tool shed and a shed that housed the pigeons. We often had bonfires, and my dad would wrap a potato in tin foil to place on the fire.

My family were poor. I wore clothes handed down by Brand, and we would excitedly open maybe one or two gifts at Christmas. I was eleven years old when Christmas gifts ended, but I never really felt poor. I had only known the life I had, my belly was always full, and my mother, Daffney, was an outstanding cook. My mum worked part-time at a video hire shop called Pick-a-Tape in Portchester, and my dad worked for McNicholas and other construction firms. In the household lived my parents, Arren, Brand and me. My sister Vikki and her children lived in Portsmouth, as did my brother Elijah and his two kids. Vikki lived in Buckland, a well-known druggy hot spot with Kayleigh and Danni. Elijah was in a flat across the park with Skye and Miclayla.

When off school, we didn't eat lunch at all. At Wicor School, I received free school dinners, and they were delicious. My favourite was a Cornish pasty and chips, followed by either a Fox's Classic Bar or a mint chocolate ice-cream ripple tub. We couldn't afford any school trips or Nike trainers like the other kids, so we had to settle for Nicks trainers. Imagine a hard plastic that would not bend strapped to the bottom of your feet; that is exactly what Nicks trainers were like! My family went to car boot sales, and that is where we would buy our biscuits from. A broken box of biscuits was a dream, as some had chocolate on them.

I only realised we were poor when on a school swimming outing as we passed by the large houses along Cams Hill in Portchester.

This kid, Byron, turned to me and said, "Nick lives in that big house over there, I bet you could never afford that, and you live in a council house."

Byron was correct; we never could afford to live there, but his mate Nick was ugly as pig shit, so I didn't care.

At Halloween, my family would take a Guy Fawkes dummy for penny for a guy to earn enough money, ready for Christmas chocolate shopping. We also collected rubbish tin cans for cash. My mother had this magnet, and if it stuck to the tin can, you would get money for them. I am sure there are worse off children than us; we had a nice house, a big garden, clothes, and food in our stomachs.

To me, I was an average girl in a council house with normal parents. My mum was a worker, and my dad was a shirker. My father liked to drink; he was from a big family in Derry in Northern Ireland. My father would answer the phone with a half bark noise like a dog would make. He said it was to not let on that an Irishman lived in the house. I never knew my granddad, as he sadly passed away before

I was born. Nor did I remember my trips to Ireland, but I had an Aunt Bryony and an Uncle Terry that he spoke of. My dad was always telling me stories of his childhood that would make the hairs on my arm stand on end.

I was never made to go to church or pray to God. My father never once spoke of religion to me unless it was involved in one of his stories. My dad attended a school with priests and nuns; he would share horror stories of how they beat him and lashed him. I would always ask him why he never told his parents of their abuse, and he would simply say that if he did, his parents would give him another punishment for it.

I always believed we were not alone, for I felt the presence of others. I could not always see them, but I knew they were there. I became scared of silly things, like going to the toilet, as I feared THEY might be watching. So, it would appear that I continued to wet my bed often until the age of nine or ten. I had started to experience dreams that I could not shake. They were usually scary ones, and the day I started to realise that some of my dreams had come to fruition was absolutely terrifying.

The first dream that brought me to this realisation was not a scary or tragic one; I dreamt that a new family had moved in across the street. This was the eighties, so any person of colour was thought of as exotic. The family was Indian, and they started to unpack their items and boxes. I remember watching them while thinking I knew this would happen as I had dreamt it. I became friends with the young boy who did not speak English; I helped him at school as he was made to sit alone at the front of the class with no interpreter. Our friendship did not last long as we soon got into a fight inside his house, so I gave him a Chinese burn and ran as fast as I could. My mother was a crazy-ass woman who was never scared of a bit of violence, and she must have been told by Brand what had happened. In the middle of the street was this poor woman who was demonstrating on her son what I had done to him: pulling his hair and grabbing his arm. My mother became enraged and tried her hardest to defend me, but the language barrier was too much, and the disagreement soon fizzled out. It was after this time all my dreams became a puzzle for me to solve, as I needed to understand them. I believed I was being sent messages and premonitions, but from who?

The next dream that sent the fear of God into me was one about my family being captured, and I had to decide who would die. My choices were my father or my mother, and I always chose my father to die. I would usually wake up crying aloud, with my father stroking my face. It was like a kick in the chest. I would sob so hard for my father dying, yet it was he who would comfort me when I awoke. I was convinced that my father would die; I also believed that it would be through some fault of mine that this would happen. Luckily, I never did get captured and have to choose between my parents, although I did, years later, have to choose between them when they split up. Many years after, I would then choose again whether I would see my father or not, and later again be faced with a police matter and a choice to let him back into my life or not. As a nineteen-year-old girl, I finally made a choice not to see my father. It was two years later, when I decided to bring him back into my life, that I discovered that he was dead.

Looking back, I can analyse the dream and make it fit into the events that would unfold. If truth be told, my dream predictions were usually more immediate. So, on this occasion, I will choose to believe that the nightmare as a child was just that: a nightmare of a young girl.

My other insights as a child were instant knowledge and feelings. I could be near a person and feel a certain way, and I knew whether the feelings were mine or theirs. I would often get a feeling about a person, and I would know if they were trouble. For me, this was normal. It always had been, so therefore it always would be. Little did I know then how much of this skill I would have and how I would come to use it in the future.

I grew up playing netball, and I spent most of my time with my best friend, Jane. She lived next door and had a busy household. Jane was the eldest sibling, then her younger sister Katy, their brother Aden, sister Selena, and the youngest, Amy. Jane's mum Janine was a bit of a whore, if I am honest, and she always had a new man in the house. They had many animals, including Alsatian dogs, snakes, rabbits, birds and more. It was a circus in the house on most days, but both exciting and fun.

Living in Portchester was great, and most children spent their days at the castle or the shoreline. Portchester Community Centre was at the centre of many things, as it had this amazing playground with a roundabout game and swings. The monkey bars were a great way to smash your knees up, and with a big field nearby, it was always an adventure.

I must have been seven years of age when I was introduced to a girl's cousin, she was much older than me, and she was tall. She had blonde hair, and most of all, she had breasts. She was from a bad neighbourhood called Kenwood. It was this girl who taught me how to use a Ouija board. Of course, it was all nonsense, and it only worked when she did it, which says a lot, really. With a bit of chalk found on the ground, she drew letters in a circle and the words yes and no. Using a glass taken from one of the kid's houses, she called upon ghosts to possess the glass and communicate with us. We would ask the ghost questions and wait for the glass to move. It was a crazy and dangerous game. Looking back now, I always knew she had moved the glass with her fingers, as it only worked when she was in charge. I have never touched a Ouija board since - not only because I never felt drawn to them but also because I simply didn't need one. Not long after, I stopped being that girl's friend for two reasons. Reason one is because she stole my Barbie doll, and reason two is because I once kissed her in my brother's bedroom. I fondled her breasts out of curiosity, and it was consensual, but I felt strange afterwards.

Every child in Portchester knew the ghost story of Charlotte White ... Charlotte White's gravestone stood in the graveyard just across from where it all happened. On the top of the castle, with her baby in her arms and a dog on the lead, is where the horrific accident took place. At exactly midnight, you can witness her ghost re-enact the events that unfolded. The dog jumps over the ledge, and as Charlotte is pulled to the edge, her baby falls from her arms to its death in the moat below. Charlotte White, in absolute despair, jumps after the baby. They say you can hear the baby crying as it floats along the moat after.

The ghost story may or may not be true. I know her grave is there, but I damn well never had the balls to rock up at midnight and find out! As kids, we would place a penny by her grave, close our eyes and walk around her headstone saying "Charlotte White, Charlotte White, Charlotte White," and the coin would always disappear.

Apart from dear Charlotte White and Tits Magee, who taught me about Ouija boards, I never had any outsiders tell me about spirits or the supernatural. Yet I recall placing playing cards into a cross shape and the remaining cards face down in the middle. At age eight, I would put my hand over the card deck and wait for images or instant knowledge to tell me which card I would turn over next. I was correct 99% of the time; this impressed me. I developed this skill and started using the red cards for positive and the black cards for negative. I had never seen this in a film or been taught about cards. As a young girl with no self-knowledge or spiritual training, I had started using ordinary playing cards for a supernatural use.

I am not one to use words like destiny, but how can a child who has a Catholic father and no influence from adults about clairvoyance suddenly teach herself a new skill? To pick up a deck of cards that had previously only been used for ordinary card games and use them for something psychic?

Chapter 2

As an educated and experienced adult, I believe we are all on this earth to learn and heal. It is only in solid form can we truly experience certain aspects of growth. Along this path, we may encounter unplanned and tragic events that leave a lasting effect on us. It is then that we return to heal, and on this next journey, more baggage is claimed. Therefore, the merry-go-round ride continues to hold us, and return again we must. I am often asked if certain people are destined to be clairvoyants or to work for spirit, and my simple answer would be yes. I believe that certain souls are more developed than others, making them an obvious choice, or their advanced journey makes them tied and bound to work for spirit. I also know that anyone can learn these skills; each and every person can hone their skills and develop them. Instead of the word destiny, maybe we should replace it with chosen, as a person may have come to this earth plane having already chosen to heal and guide others spiritually.

As time went by for me as a child, I had further evidence of supernatural gifts, but the gifts became dark and scary through actions of my own.

It was 1994 when my mother decided it was time to pack up our troubles and move to a large house in Paulsgrove. Paulsgrove is an interesting place: many people are related, and the area used to be well known for scallywags at the time. Hardened criminals, thieves and paedophiles were placed in the area, along with violent residents and crazy-ass kids.

I dreaded the move. I did not want to leave my home and friends in Portchester at all, but the idea of being allowed to catch the bus to school excited me. I was still attending Wicor Primary School, and all kids there feared "Paulsgrovers," as they were known then.

The day I first viewed my new house, it was an adventure. With a chalk pit behind the house, it looked like something out of a film. It was not quite the White Cliffs of Dover, but it was magnificent to stare up at it. I would later realise that it was good that I liked the chalk so much, as white water from the tap was an obvious sign that I would drink it for the next several bloody years. The property was huge, with four big bedrooms, a dining room, kitchen, lounge and garden. The garden was home to many stray cats, large evil-looking ones; it was like a Stephen King scene from Pet Cemetery ... FREAKY!

I chose the first bedroom at the top of the stairs; little did I know that I had chosen the exact room that harboured a dark and disturbing secret. I was happy to know that children lived next door; with only Brand to play with, I was not optimistic about fun and games lying ahead. Next door was a young girl, and they had broken toys and half-built vehicles everywhere; it was like a dirty old junkyard. When I first spoke with the little girl, all she wanted to know was which room was mine. As I pointed to my bedroom window, she ran away.

As time moved by, I started to realise catching the bus with all the local children wasn't as much fun as I thought; the King Richard's kids hated everyone. My teachers disliked my new tardiness too, but buses would often be full to the brim, or they simply wouldn't risk coming up the hill to my stop in icy weather.

My new house smelt strange; there were nails in the carpets and fleas everywhere! Mother looked at it as a challenge, a fixer-upper. I looked at it as pig shit. With the houses built on such a steep hill, the foundations were shifting. I could poke my hand through a wall, the walls split, and the ceilings travelled away from their original place. It was a shit hole!

We slept in each other's rooms while mother waved her magic wand and decorated, so it was a few weeks before I actually slept in my own chosen room. I would often run up the stairs and see a glimpse of a man, but in a flash, he was gone. I had become used to seeing spirits or hearing a child laugh.

My room had a beautiful dark pink carpet and mint green wallpaper, and I hung my dolphin pictures with pride. On my dresser opposite my bed, I stood up my few but treasured cassettes. That carpet, or the carpet from hell as I soon started to call it, was the bane of my existence. My dog Charlie, a Yorkshire Terrier breed, would zoom around my room, and every paw and footprint would leave a dark patch. The stupid carpet had to be hoovered in one direction; otherwise, it looked a totally different colour! I am anal when it comes to cleaning; some may describe me as a super bitch from hell sergeant major. I can place all this on my mother. She awakes and is up by five o'clock cleaning. She does her hair and make-up, and then boom, the house is done. As children, we would wake up, and God help us if we tried to sit on the sofa. Mother would scream, "I have just smoothed that!" Once the house had been cleaned, no mess was allowed, and all ornaments were polished daily. A normal deep clean that happens a few times a year in other households was a daily regime in ours.

I would often walk into my room and see a bum print on my bed, like when you sit on the bed. I would go to sleep at night, and my bed would move up and down. I remember thinking this is comforting, like a ride at the fair. I could be in my room, and my cassettes would knock over for no reason. The air would turn ice cold, and I would get this eerie feeling that someone was watching me. I never really minded all of this, but the thing that actually scared me was my stupid dog. At night when I lay in bed, my dog would run into the room and charge at the corner of darkness, growling and snarling. The growls would turn into a bark, followed by whimpers before he would run out of the room. As a child, this was disturbing, and I knew that if I opened my eyes, I would see him: the man that I sometimes saw on the stairs.

In the nineties, people still took camera films to the local photo shop to be developed, and my mother loved to take before and after photos of the new house. A local worker for the council congratulated my mother on her ability to transform a council property into something spectacular. It was my mother's photos that revealed another supernatural mystery. The photos of my room contained pictures of faces in the dolphin frames. I had three wonderful A3 landscape pictures of dolphins, one above my bed and two opposite on the wall. The one above where I slept had a face in the photo, as clear as day for all to see. The face was not of my mother or of another who lived in the house, and it then appeared in the other photos of my bedroom too.

My mother was working in North End, managing a charity shop. She was the first manager to turn over thousands of pounds in one week, so she was well-respected there. She still kept in contact with the lady who we did a council exchange with, and it was the photos of my bedroom that led her to reach out to this lady. I overheard my mother and sister Vikki talking.

My mum whispered, "Madie said that he hung himself in Bryony's bedroom …"

So here I was, sleeping in the room where a man had hung himself. No wonder the girl next door wanted to know which room was mine!

Life in Paulsgrove was complicated: everyone knew everyone, and if your face didn't fit, then, well, you'd better run.

As my mother was happy with the house and it didn't seem like we were moving anytime soon, the next few years living there were interesting. Most nights, I would endure my dog's antics, I became complacent with a bouncy bed each night, and eventually, I laid my cassettes down.

My life soon changed, for my mother became friends with Dave. Dave was a psychic/medium, and we all soon came to call him … psychic Dave! Not very imaginative, I know, but it does what it says on the tin. Dave was a gypsy, and he often visited my mum at her shop. He soon became a volunteer and her close friend. When we first met, he would just stare at me, and I studied his face in return. He wore glasses and had loads of blackheads that I wanted to pick; disgusting, I know, but I love a good spot. His skin was olive in colour, and he had piercing blue eyes. He wore jeans and a top like an average man. However, Dave was not average, for he knew things.

He once stopped me in my tracks by saying, "spirit children jump up and down on your bed at night."

It was not a question; it was a statement of fact, and he followed on with, "You see spirits too."

Dave being my friend, was like having the keys to the kingdom. I would question him endlessly for hours, asking him about the spirit world and, more importantly, how can humans exist? I was obsessed; I needed to know why and how humans can exist, when we were taught from day one that to make something, you need the ingredients. The earth, the trees, my thoughts and feelings and the spirit world; how?

Maybe people ponder human existence; some may discuss the big bang and how the planet was born. I was stumped from another angle. Believing 100% in the spirit world, I was confused. The spirit world and souls, energy and other planes were not explainable with science. If you want a cake, you must have the ingredients. For the earth to form, gases and minerals were required. We are taught that you cannot make something out of nothing, so, in my mind, I felt nothing should exist. This question burned inside me; it drove me crazy at night and during the day.

When I asked Dave this question, and I pressed him to answer, he simply said, "One day, you will tell me the answer."

And years later, in a snooker hall on Kingston Crescent, I did exactly that.

One of my simpler and earlier enquiries was to ask how does the spirit world separate spirits' levels of growth? Dave informed me that the light shines so bright that a spirit would not be able to see if they tried to enter a level above their own development. I also asked, where do bad people go? Is there a hell as such? I was informed there are lower planes just as there are higher planes. Later in life, I travelled to one of these lower planes, guided by a very gifted spiritual teacher named Paul. It was Paul who helped me in my darkest times. He guided me, and over the years, I have often returned to him for help.

I was still very young when I met Dave. He did predict that I had the sight and ability to work for spirit, and I continued to have my dreams that would come true. While working at my mum's shop, a new supernatural encounter started. I would be walking through to the stock room, and my top would be tugged on.

It wasn't long before Dave said to me, "Do you feel your top being tugged like this?" Dave continued to demonstrate on himself, and once I nodded in agreement, he informed me it was spirit children playing with me. It was the norm for me, spirit children jumping on my bed, to see spirits through the day and for my top to be pulled. It was all so normal.

My grandad George lived on the Isle of Wight in a place called Ryde. A few times a year, we would descend to the dock and travel on the catamaran from Portsmouth Hard to Ryde. It was beautiful and such a treat to sit on the boat and then walk the wooden pier slats to land. Never as a child did I ever catch the train from the boat to land, we always walked. We would then climb the longest hill through Ryde High Street. It was very far for a child to trek, but I guess the bus was expensive. The Isle of Wight was a dream; every day was like a Sunday. Slow and quiet streets, shops and food for tourists were along every cobbled road, and the arcades were in abundance. We never went inside, but it was still fun to watch. The smells of the salty sea air and fish and chips were intoxicating. It is strange to think that I never swam in the sea or walked along the beach with ice cream, yet it was still paradise to me.

My grandad was an avid gardener; he had been a porter at St Mary's hospital, along with my nan, Billie who was a staff nurse there. George had served in the Royal Air Force, and my nan was in the Women's Royal Air Force (WRAF); she served for a few years. My nan was the first woman to carry two large machine guns, one on each shoulder. A picture of this was printed in the Daily Mirror, and George served from the Second World War until the war ended. My great-grandad, named Frank Doleman, also served in the Scottish Royal Guard; he was captured in a POW camp during WWI. As punishment, they would bury them in the ground, leaving only their heads above the dirt. My great-grandad made a cunning plan to escape. He arranged for their group of prisoners to call in the guards by faking illness; they then all attacked the guards and escaped. However, they were soon caught and returned to the camp for punishment.

When my nan was in the WRAF, she worked in electrical communications, climbing telephone poles. She later entered the entertainment section, and she performed with George Formby. George Formby was a famous ukulele player known all over the world. My nan would dance, and she won a cup named The Victor Sylvester Cup in the 1940s. For anyone born after a certain date, that cup would be equivalent to winning a cup from Strictly Come Dancing.

In the 1960s, my grandad George walked the Isle of Wight for charity, roughly around 80 miles. My grandad and nan were part of the Church of England, and they took my mother, Daffney, to church every Sunday. My grandparents were well known and liked. George once witnessed a gentleman bus inspector called Pat be hit by a train on Ryde Esplanade. My grandad pulled his body out from under the train and retrieved his severed arm before the ambulance arrived. Pat survived the ordeal, but he did lose his arm. None of my family from the Isle of Wight heard voices or nor did they see any spirits; they displayed no gifts of a supernatural nature.

I awoke one morning from a terrible dream; I had dreamt of my grandad. He stood in a field holding a baby, it was night-time, and there was a pub nearby. The pub had lights on and many people inside, but my grandad just stood there, rocking this baby and looking at me. I knew what this meant; he was not long for this world. Dreams are not an exact science; deciphering any dream is not easy. Even at a young age, I associated babies with a passing and a death as a new beginning. I shared this dream with my mother, as did she with Dave; Dave also knew what this meant. My grandad was taken into hospital before this dream had been put upon me. He was recovering well, so maybe my dream was wrong?

My mother never remembers any of her dreams, but I recall her having a reoccurring dream about a bus. She would wake up at three in the morning every time she had this dream, and it was unusual for my mother ever to recall any dream. Dave predicted that my grandad would be taken into hospital and that my mother would never make it there in time to say goodbye. My grandad sadly passed away, but my mother did make it in time to say her goodbyes.

Not long after, my dream predictions would send me another warning. I had formed a lovely friendship with a volunteer from my mother's charity shop. Dot was so kind and warm; she was in her eighties and was short, with blue eyes and white curly short hair. Dot always cuddled me and really spoilt me with affection. I remember Dot living in a flat on New Road with a glass roof. I had often taken my dog to see her; she loved Charlie. One day Dot did not come to work. I was worried as we had received no telephone call, which was not like her at all. I sat at home worrying; I was waiting for my mother to call me with an update. Earlier that morning, I had shared my dream of the night before, telling my mother that Dot was sadly dead. My mother dismissed me, and later that day, she called me.

My mother said, "Dot is fine. We have found her."

I knew this was a lie.

That evening, at around six o'clock, I heard the key in the door, and my mother had returned from work. She looked at me, I started to cry, and she confessed.

"Yes, she is gone, baby. I just didn't want to tell you over the phone."

She opened her arms, and I hugged my mother so tight. My Dot was gone, just like I had known ever since I opened my eyes that morning.

Chapter 3

The year was 1997 when my mother announced that we were to move house again; she had found a flat somewhere else in Paulsgrove. I never understood why we were moving to a ground floor flat or from a four-bedroom house to a three-bed. As I stared up at this building of flats, several adults and a flock of children stared back at me. The first-floor balcony seemed to be a hot spot for residents to sit and drink. The street was called Cheltenham Road, and the building was named Cotswold, but the view was nothing like the name implied.

Our flat was long; the hallway stretched for at least fifty metres, with rooms and doors leading off like a centipede's legs. The shape of the corridor was like a lightning bolt; as you approached a sharp corner, the carpet took a direct turn to the end of the hallway. My brother Brand later discovered that the unusual layout was because the whole block of flats was once all shops. The flat had fleas, and the stench of piss and dust was intense. My brothers took up the front room carpet and walked it through the lounge doors that led onto a small, concrete front garden. This idea was a lot better than walking the carpet through the length of the corridor and out of the front door. Brand and Arren left the stinky, wet, old, musty carpet balanced on the waist-high wall. By the time they had walked back through the flat and out of the front door, the carpet had been nicked! Who the hell would be vile enough to steel that mangy carpet? How quick and desperate they must have been was beyond me, but welcome to Paulsgrove indeed.

I hated living in that shit hole of a flat; I couldn't even stand walking to the corner shop. I was a teenager, and I had a nice body and a pleasant face, a face that would turn red whenever I approached the balcony of men who would stare and whistle. We did have a nice neighbour, though, called Sharon. Sharon had short hair, a loud mouth, and a big heart. My mum and Sharon started a friendship and soon became good mates. Sharon lived with her daughter and young son; their flat was similar to ours but messier. To be fair, everyone's house was messier than ours; not everyone had a rigid cleaning process like my mum.

It was Sharon who asked me to perform my first ever proper reading. Sharon would say she was a White Witch. At the time, I did not understand this or know what it really meant. I was only thirteen the day her young daughter came running into our flat.

"Mum has seen a ghost!" she exclaimed. "She said you need to come quickly."

I walked into Sharon's flat, not knowing what to expect or who I might see. As Sharon dragged hard on her Red Band cigarette, she explained to me what had taken place. In her kitchen, Sharon was unloading the washing machine, and her youngest boy had run past.

As Sharon shouted out to him, "Get back to bed," he ignored her.

Annoyed and angry, Sharon charged down the hallway, but he had disappeared. Confused and vexed, Sharon then walked back on herself to open her son's bedroom door, only to find him fast asleep in his bed. Sharon was shaken up by the whole ordeal, and she wanted answers.

She asked me to ask the presence who it was and what it wanted? I had no idea what I was doing, nor did I have any type of training for this.

I settled my mind and walked up and down the hallway, looking for a spirit; I eventually sat down and listened. I then proceeded to relay to Sharon any information that entered my mind. You could hear a pin drop with the silence, the air was cold, and I could smell the smoke from her cigarette.

I opened my mouth. "I have a young child here, she said she dances on your bed, and you sometimes know that she is here."

Sharon gasped before telling me, "YES, my bed moves during the night."

I felt pleased that she understood this, so I continued, "I feel she is yours. Do you understand this?"

Sharon's eyes were wide, and I swear she had stopped blinking, but she nodded. I finished my reading with a parting message, saying that she just wants you to know that she is here and she is Karrera's twin.

Sharon confirmed with me many years later that the information I had shared from a twin spirit child had been confirmed to her by another medium.

I had previously made comments and known information that I should not have known, but this was in my own time and on most occasions, I said things without even realising. That night I had purposefully aimed to ask questions and contact the dead, so how did I know the information? I will explain it as best as I can. I let myself be aware of the cold chill and the presence in the room. I cleared my thoughts and focused on my mind's eye. When I asked the spirit world questions in my head, I received instant knowledge as answers. It is difficult to explain how I knew the knowledge as answers were not my own thoughts, but at times, the large amount of knowledge coming in an instant helped me distinguish it.

I needed to know more about my ability, and I wanted to be trained, but psychic Dave felt I was too young. I did then have another encounter with a spirit. I had usually seen spirits in many forms. I had witnessed a glimpse, but in a flash, the person was gone; I also saw spirits as shadows or in my mind's eye. The spirits always disappeared in a flash, too fast to really study them. It had always been obvious they were dead. I would see them, but they were almost see-through, like a trick of the light.

At Cheltenham Road, in our newly decorated flat, I witnessed for the first time a spirit so real that I mistook him to be alive. I was walking through my long hallway towards the front door, and I was just about to turn left and then around the corner to a sharp right. As I turned the corner, I jumped backwards. Standing in front of me was a tall man wearing a cream knitted jumper. The man had hair parted down the centre; his hair was dark brown and hung straight to his chin length. He was a white man, wearing black trousers. I could not see through him. I looked him up and down, and he looked down at me.

I said aloud, "Who the hell are you?"

The unknown man then disappeared; he looked young - early twenties in age or a very tall lad in his late teens.

I volunteered at my mum's charity shop, first on a Saturday, but soon I was kept off school to work there full time. I missed school, even though I had nothing in common with the other kids at Portchester Secondary School. I was very intelligent and gifted. Unfortunately, I was always fighting and being beyond my age in mind. I gave my teachers a run for their money in arguments. My passion was sport; I loved all games from Netball to Track and anything competitive. I played Goal Attack on the Netball team, just as I had at Wicor School, and I still love sport now.

I did not connect with many kids at my school; their problems were tiny in comparison to mine.

My mum would sit us down and say, "Kids, we cannot afford the rent, so we are going to be homeless. Which one of you has run up the phone bill?"

As Brand and I sat on the sofa in silence, listening to my mum explain that we would have nowhere to live, it was a dark time for us. My dad's drinking and threats had gotten out of hand, and my mother had grown tired of him taking what little we had. He would go on a bender and usually take our bill money with him. Eventually, my mother kicked him out, but he would still call, threatening to kill my brother Elijah. His favourite was to threaten my other siblings, saying he would crack them from behind over the head with a brick and then kill them. My dad also liked to tell my mum that he would knife her. These threats would be either in writing or left on the landline answering machine. The police did nothing; they just said to call them when he does it!

I was in therapy as a teenager; I guess certain parts of my childhood really did take their toll on me. As a young girl, I remember opening my brother's window, climbing up onto the window ledge and planning to jump. At the large house in Paulsgrove, I would stand at the window looking out of the net curtain, crying, wanting to die and to leave this world behind.

My life consisted of a busy mother who always worked, an alcoholic father and all the crazy life challenges that arose along the way. I could never do it, though, no matter how much comfort it gave me to plan my own death. I could never leave my nieces behind in a cruel world with no protector. No matter how dark my world became, I could never leave them behind; I needed to stay in case they wanted my help. In Wicor School, the classrooms had become overcrowded, so they had to move a few of the more advanced students up a year. I had spent time learning with the older children, and in Portchester School, a few teachers noticed my potential too.

I would work at the charity shop, missing the few friends that I had, while slowly being forgotten about by my mates. Eventually, the phone stopped ringing, and my best friend Leanne left to attend another school, as she said I was never at school with her anyway. I would catch the number 1A bus from Paulsgrove to North End. I hated the bus, although I did like the thinking time. I was like a sponge when sitting on the bus, so I always tried to sit away from others. I recall sitting by the window just minding my own business. The glass had all steamed up, so it must have been wintertime. I felt the seat go down as someone sat next to me; I didn't turn towards them as I had no reason to. I felt an extreme sadness infecting my body and mind; I also knew the person was female. The lady was a rape victim; a family member had abused her. What use was this information to me? The feelings were hers; they were not mine, and neither was the knowledge I was soaking up into my mind. The pain belonged to her;

it was not for me to hold onto. My teacher and friend Paul speaks about living with sensitivity, referring to the spirit world and energies. As a young girl who was not trained on how to protect herself, I was open and received waves of energies crashing into me. Unwanted and not needed, I was a stranger to this lady. I was also riding the bus early in the morning. Even as a child, I understood that there was a time and a place for supernatural work, and that time was not now.

I suffered a great deal with the invasions on my body and mind, thoughts and feelings that belonged to others. I found loud and fast-paced environments to be an overload at times; I would become irritable, dizzy, and anxious. This was a big learning curve for me, for I encouraged the knowledge at first. I would sit in a room of people and ask questions in my head. This was good with friends as they found it interesting to test me to see what I could "GUESS" correctly. I soon realised that testing my abilities with strangers was pointless, as the energy and communication would flow from the spirit world to me, and this would then need to flow to the correct person. When I held onto the information and could not pass it on, the process would not be completed. I did start to notice that when I did pick up on others' emotions and unintentionally tuned into their energy, it was usually deep hurt and pain. I did not know why; maybe pain and emotional turmoil were the types of pain I recognised the most?

I do believe now that certain mediums are better suited to particular people. This is why a friend can claim that a medium was rubbish while another may say they were good. I was always drawn to pain and darkness; maybe this is because I could empathise with them and offer messages from a place of understanding. Not everyone is suited to the same medium, I have found some mediums to be great, but they have not told me anything meaningful. Relaying messages from the spirit world is a complex task; I believe this process is perhaps slightly easier if the medium has had experiences similar to the sitter. A reading is a mixture of the medium providing evidence of an authentic link, messages from loved ones and healing. Healing can begin with the sitter breaking down in tears and releasing emotions. The medium may offer guidance and advice; I truly feel that we grow and develop as humans from challenging experiences. It is from these lessons that we offer advice and guidance to our own friends and loved ones; we are wiser because we have grown and learned. As a medium, we may need to deliver delicate information and tread on paths less trodden. Imagine the sensitive task of supporting a domestic violence victim and passing on messages from loved ones. Grieving parents, a rape victim or a child of abuse may all cross your path requesting a reading. Any person who sits for a medium has come for a reason; they either are curious or need guidance or proof of the afterlife. On many occasions, people feel lost and are in need of direction, or maybe their question is simply to ask whether their partner is cheating and banging Janine the whore from number 31!

I did notice a pattern when I grew older with my supernatural friends; I had sitters drawn to me with similar pasts. My best friend Mercedes always picked up on a person's shopping habits and hot beverage preferences. Leanne would speak about animals and healing when we would all read the same sitter. Mercedes is a girly girl; she would mention relationships and how people felt about others at their place of work. A pattern was obvious to me during readings; I noticed that mediums would usually discuss similar pasts or similar interests, although this could just have been a coincidence.

Chapter 4

My life was taking a new path. After years of working at various charity shops, I had dark times ahead of me. My mother's chats of being homeless had taken their toll, and then one day, while visiting my father, a new lie was sprung. Near Commercial Road shops in Portsmouth's town centre, homeless alcoholics would sit on the benches drinking and stinking.

Can you imagine the embarrassment for a young girl to be shopping with friends and then for someone to laugh and say, "Isn't that your dad on that bench?"

I would always retort with a big, fat "NO!"

Sadly, it usually was my dad, smoking his rolled cigarettes and drinking beer with the local homeless men. He would hardly notice me as I hurried by with my schoolmates.

My mother had kicked my dad out; somehow, he had managed to weasel his way into a live-in security job in town. The job conveniently included a caravan and was central to many pubs. I hated going to see him; my visits usually consisted of us walking from pub to pub and listening to his ramblings. My dad truly believed that he would appear on the TV Show *Stars in Their Eyes*. He would sing, and my mother would take him back. Never mind the threats to kill or his drinking antics.

A low point for me was sitting in my dad's dirty, messy caravan while he showed me his cassettes and song lyrics. We spoke about how he would sing a song released by a black man, but my dad felt that the make-up artists would blacken out his face for TV. For dinner, he had bought a cooked chicken. I watched in disgust as my dad urinated in his wash bucket. With wide eyes and a wrinkled nose from the smell, I watched in shock as he dipped his hands in the same bucket that he had just urinated in. My father then washed his hands in a mixture of dirty dishwater and warm piss; how has his life come to this? As my father then proceeded to strip the chicken he had bought for dinner with his piss hands, I gave dinner a hard pass.

The caravan was situated in a car park under a building, a shared car park for Trotters Cafe, a Bowling Alley, Hairdressers, and a Music shop. We walked into the cafe, and I was curious. My dad never spent any money on me, and that included buying breakfast or lunch. I was thrust upon some lady and my dad turned on the charm, informing her that I was at college and looking for work. The lady never spoke to me, and as their conversation continued, I thought to myself, 'Surely, she can see I am only thirteen?' Well, how wrong I was, as I was offered a Saturday job as a waitress to start that weekend.

I never minded working at Trotters, I was a fast learner, and I could turn my hand to anything. I was happy only to earn fifteen pounds for the whole day, and after buying a pack of ten fags and paying the £1.60 bus fare from Paulsgrove, I then gave the remaining £10.00 to mother. However, I hated the smell. I would ride the bus with people commenting on the stench, and it was me they were referring to. Working in a cafe had the perk of free food, but the smell infected your pores and hair like a virus.

I made new friends while working at cafe; Kelly and Emily were great girls. I was pretending to be older in age, but although they never questioned me, they did wonder why I never went clubbing with them. I did go to the pubs, though. At thirteen years of age, I was served drinks in shops and pubs. I am not sure if it was my confidence or looks, but let's just say that I didn't mind either way.

I was soon promoted to working the cash register, which was fast-paced and hectic; after this, I was trained to cook. A normal day started at 6 am with a bus ride to Portsmouth town. I was trusted with cash to shop at 7 am at Tesco for the cafe, and by 8 am, I was prepping food and frying breakfasts. Not many could handle the pressure, but I was fine. It wasn't long before a new manager took over, and he said he would want me to take over the business, plus he wanted me to work there full time. I had school to go to, but he thought I only attended college on a Monday, thanks to my dad's lies. My mother needed the money, so that was the decision made: I started working in the cafe full time.

I was earning up to £160.00 a week, which was a lot of money for a young girl in 1997. I gave most of the money to my mum, but I could stretch my money to go far and wide. I spent my days working in the cafe, and I started sleeping overnight at my sister Vikki's. My sister lived in Buckland near the town, so I was closer to work, and it saved me the bus fare from Paulsgrove. My life started to change; I would spend my evenings at the Snooker Club, drinking and smoking. I would meet Emily for drinks at a local pub, and I started seeing boys. Any distraction from my home life was welcomed.

My sister lived in a three-bedroom flat, and it was there, at Vikki's house, that I would see the lady. The front door was an ugly dark grey, and as you walked through it, the kitchen was directly on the left and opposite it was the stairs. The lounge was at the back of the flat overlooking the street. I always hated my niece's bedroom. Kayleigh and Danni shared a room, and I would usually top and tail with Kayleigh when I stayed over. My sister left the hallway light on, but as I lay in bed, I would always feel there was someone out on the landing. The bedroom door was ajar, with just a big enough gap for me to see through. The spirit would walk past the door and stand at the top of the stairs. She wore a long nightdress and had an angry look on her face. I would close my eyes tight shut, repeating words over in my head in an attempt to ignore her presence.

I soon became tired of the bitching and arguing at Trotters, and I applied for a job at Port Solent Marina. I was canvassing the restaurants and bars with my CV in hand when a handsome manager at Pasta Factory restaurant offered me an interview on the spot. I impressed him with my experience, and although I had applied to wash dishes, he stated that I was too pretty to be a kitchen porter and offered me a waitress role. The food smelt like heaven, and all staff were given new names for their badge when they started; for example, Matt would become Matteo. The Italian restaurant wanted the staff names to sound foreign, but I was not given a new name; I was allowed to keep mine. I worked my little butt off, and I was soon rewarded for my hard work; I was made the only salaried waitress. As the head waitress, I was never sent home when it was quiet, I always worked longer hours than the others, but my wage was protected.

The marina was seasonal; in the summer, it heaved, but in the winter, it had quiet patches, which is when I was taught how to cook. Everyone who worked there was usually drinking or on drugs, which was normal for hospitality. It was while working there that my childhood best friend Jane came back into my life. We were short-staffed one evening, so I telephoned my friend Jane, and she covered a shift. She was quiet and fast, so my boss offered her more hours. Jane had a falling out with her mum, and I offered for Jane to come and live with me, but I never even asked for my mother's permission.

The day that Jane moved into my house in Paulsgrove, my mother warned her, "Jane, don't you ever bring drugs into my house!"

My mum was ever so scary, and her warning was serious, so Jane was sly and hid her pills in a pair of socks stashed in my water pipe.

Jane was a deeply troubled girl, as was I, and together, we were the perfect recipe for disaster.

Life could not have been easy for my mother; I was paying her five hundred pounds a month rent, but this must have been a kick to the gut. The guilt or shame must have eaten away at her, for she frequently blew up at me; I often left the house after she went off on one. My mum was depressed. I didn't know it at the time, but I do now, thinking back. Financially my mother was struggling, she had taken me, her daughter, out of school to work full time, and I was becoming a monster. I was drinking alcohol in the house, I moved a friend in without asking, and I was hardly around.

The death of my Grandad George had hit her hard. I recall having to hide pills as she was going to take an overdose.

My mum chased me around the flat, shouting, "Where are they? Where have you fucking hid them?"

Caressing a framed picture of my grandad, it was obvious what her plan was, so I hid all the pills. In return for my help, my mother shouted profanities at me before punching me in the face. Jane would often hide in my wardrobe. I would search the flat for her and then find Jane crouched on top of my shoes like a robber. Everyone was petrified of my mum; she was crazy and pro-violent. The courts had put an order in place while I was at primary school, stating that my mum couldn't enter any public building without two male escorts!

As my home life became more miserable, I started to drink more, and I can pinpoint the exact time I knew something was adrift. It was late in the evening, and I had run out of Archers Peach Schnapp's, so I telephoned everyone I knew asking for drink. I poured every drop from all my empties and cursed the shops for being shut. It was around two in the morning, I was sixteen years old, and I knew I needed a drink.

I felt trapped at that age; I was forced to work and give my mum all my money, and my dad was useless and a threat most days. I suffered from depression myself, and my mother had turned into something completely unpredictable.

My employer, who loved me, even started to see the cracks. I often drank at work, and my new favourite was to pour Baileys into my cup of tea. I would turn up to work as drunk as a skunk but still functioning. The final nail in the coffin at work was when I had an accident that resulted in a hospital visit because of drugs. We once attended a big staff night out, and I decided to accept an offer of ecstasy. What I didn't know was that they had been dipped in acid. I had a crazy night; I pretended to fuck myself with a champagne bottle in the middle of a restaurant. I walked for miles through the streets and then spent hours watching Jane's mum Janine rock her baby back and forth.

The following day I felt like I was in a bubble and like I was walking on clouds. The escapism from drugs was welcomed by me; I kissed it and hugged it before making love to the new path I would walk down. My new love of drugs was hard and fast; I started taking speed at work, or whizz, as we called it. I would take pills, smoke weed and drink as much alcohol as I could handle. I, unfortunately, took to this like a duck to water, but one night at work, it was my downfall. Jane was on a date with one of the chefs from the kitchen; she had taken pills and invited me to party with her after my shift. As I was cleaning the bar, she threw an empty glass of wine at me, and I caught it like a boss. I had cut my finger deep, so I bandaged it up with two or three wraps and off I went.

As I partied through the night, I always held my index finger in the air, but it kept bleeding through. I rocked back and forth, wondering why it would never stop bleeding. The next day, I walked to Queen Alexandra hospital to be checked out, and I still have the scar to this day. My mother received a telephone call from my boss stating that I had missed a shift at work, which would be unpaid. My mother argued with my boss demanding that I still be paid. This was when he informed her that the accident happened at work, but I was on drugs which is why the finger would not stop bleeding. My mum did not react to this news of my drug use.

Instead, she retorted, "Well, it happened on your property, so she should still be paid!"

I lost my job after this, but they did pay me my salary and an extra one thousand pounds! I assume the money was for my silence, but who knows?

I needed money, so I took on many agency jobs. It was hard to be taken seriously when trying to convince an agency that a sixteen-year-old girl was reliable. I would explain my rent and bill outgoings, stating that my financial commitments would make me more reliable than half the other twats walking in the door.

I worked in an ice cream factory at Hilsea and a plant bulb factory too. I attended the bulb factory with Jane and my sister Vikki; I made it to 9 am before popping some pills. With my eyes as wide as saucers and packing bulbs into plant pots, I couldn't understand why everyone didn't take pills every day of their life?

I was jumping from one job to the next, including a paper factory that was so boring I thought about suicide from paper cuts. I eventually landed a job at Hampshire Cosmetics, a factory in Waterlooville. It may as well have been in China because I didn't drive. Each morning I walked in the cold to Allaway Avenue to our collection point with Jane; we would be transported to work and charged £13.50 a week for it. The year was 2000/2001, and we sat on the minibus sipping our Orange Fanta laced with speed, chatting shit with the others. Even as an alcoholic child who took drugs daily, I still would experience the supernatural.

That morning, I whispered to Jane, "That guy with the hoodie is going to ask you for drugs. Say no."

Jane and I sold drugs, or swapped drugs may be a more accurate description. We would swap DVDs for the broken bottom pills of a 1000-piece bag. After, we would walk to Jane's dad and swap the crushed pills for speed. Jane was used to my supernatural antics. Since childhood, I would warn her of my dreams, and many of them came true.

That day at the factory, I was working on line eleven, I looked up, and Jane came running across the factory.

"Bryony, that guy just asked me for pills. The exact guy that you said would!!!!!!"

I made sure Jane had not sold him any drugs or taken the conversation further before assuring her it was for the best as he was dangerous.

It was not long before Jane moved out of my mum's flat, as did I. I moved to Chichester Road in North End. I paid £65.00 a week to live in a shared house with a bunch of smackheads. My landlord offered me to either pay the rent or for Jane to sleep with him. Jane never did, so I was stuck with rent to pay; luckily, I had started a more stable career at a pizza restaurant.

Jane had moved in with her dad, a drug dealer and a very bad man. I was working and taking drugs, but the drink was still my favourite.

I was heading down a dark and ugly path, I was still connected to supernatural activities, but it was less than before. I still had the burning question inside of me that nothing should exist!

I was usually at the snooker hall drinking when one day in he walked; it was psychic Dave! It had been years since we had seen each other. I recognised his eyes immediately, a skill I still have to this day.

I can take one look at a person, and I immediately know if they are a drinker. I can also tell you if someone is a mean drunk. They can be the loveliest looking person, but the eyes never lie. Dave was no different today; he was on a bender. He sat with his pint on the bar; he kept smiling and looking at me. I asked him why he was drinking.

"You know why," he replied.

The smell of the snooker hall was sweet, of stale beer and wooden furniture; it was heaven to me. I love the smell of a pub; I find it comforting.

Dave turned to me and just waited for me to respond.

"You are drinking because nothing should exist, and you want the answer."

Dave nodded his head; his eyes looked longingly at me as he informed me that I was going to give him the answer we had both been searching for.

Without even thinking, I just opened my mouth, and the words fell out ...

"The answer does not matter; it does not matter because our brain will not understand the answer. Even if we were dead in front of the almighty power and received the answer, we wouldn't be able to understand it. On earth, we are taught earthly laws and physics, so, therefore, it would be gibberish."

A light bulb had turned on inside my head; the answer I had been seeking was given to me. I had truly contemplated that question, as had he. Seeking an answer had been obsessive; I had even considered taking my own life just so I could ask the almighty power. I daydreamed, visualising myself in a bright light, asking my heart's desire.

I never did see Dave again after that day.

If you gave birth to a child and raised the kid in a single room and only taught the child about humans, what do you think they would make of animals? Think about the sky, the sea, and the elements; if you pretended that nothing else existed, they would believe this as fact.

If, after many years, you then inform the child that there are animals with horns and fur, a wind element that blows and a sea of water that moves, would the child believe you?

Their brain would not be able to comprehend this new knowledge if they had never heard of it, seen it, or touched it with their fingertips.

Our reality and knowledge on this earth plane are what limit us; we are taught millions of scientific facts and little of magic and other possibilities. It is through the learning experience that knowledge is gained, hence why many teachers and subjects do not give you the answer but the aim or objective. We could not experience and learn to our best potential if we had all of the answers, and this is true to life. When I discovered that I would not be able to understand any given answer due to my limited knowledge on this earth, I found comfort. I also became aware of just how little we know. When I speak to the spirit world, I am just scratching the surface. The earth is our world, literally. However, what if I told you that the world was something else and the earth was like a closet in comparison? Now imagine that all we know is the closet; therefore, the closet is everything, but something much bigger and greater is just a step away. Our world and this life are just a drop in the ocean, but the ocean is more powerful than you or I could ever imagine.

Chapter 5

Spiralling out of control was my new theme in life. I had made some new acquaintances, and they were mainly drug addicts and thieves. I remember one guy trying to sell me clothes that were damp. I held the Levi jeans in my hand, wondering, 'Why the hell are they wet?' The jeans, along with the rest of the clothes, had been stolen right off a neighbour's washing line! I kept up well with all the adults; I could take three or four ecstasy tablets and still look sober. My friends consisted of just Jane; we spent most of our days working and getting off our nuts. Jane managed to land a job at a nursery. Fuck knows why they hired her; she was off her head on pills at the interview. I was working at a new restaurant as a trainer in Gunwharf Quays, and since Jane moved out of my room at Chichester Road, we spent less time together.

I soon had one of the scariest times of my life after taking way too many drugs and losing half a nipple! It started out with Brand and me going to a nightclub called Time at Southsea seafront. I wore a silver snake dress and had taken lots of speed. I was only sixteen years of age and was standing in line at Time and Envy nightclub when the bouncer asked me for proof of age. I had some fake ID on me, but when he asked me for my DOB, I just blanked. My brother Brand had entered the club, leaving me outside, so I jumped in the queue for Zoom and partied in there on my Jack Jones.

I was buzzing my tits off and telephoned Jane's dad. I knew he would have more drugs, and he did. That night was very strange. We ate some ice cream, and I had taken what I thought was a large ball of speed, but it was not speed. Her dad stroked my breast; I remember thinking, 'Did that just happen?' I brushed off the thought, as I was so off my head that I could hardly feel anything. Later on, while I was lying on the floor, he kissed me on the lips. Now, most people on drugs can end up kissing; I once French kissed Leanne at a house party in front of many. It was only a peck on the lips, so no harm was done. I had a boyfriend at the time called Tim; he was so in love with me that it was surreal.

It wasn't long before I realised I felt very unusual, Jane's dad kept trying to touch me, and I felt stupid. I felt silly as I realised that, yes, he must have stroked my breast earlier, and I had not pushed him away. He kept looking at me and grinning with this crazy smile. I didn't want to upset my main drug dealer, so I opted to say that I was on my period, hoping this would put him off me. It seemed to work. As I lay there, happy in my druggy coma, I was spaced out, a state that I enjoyed when the buzz was so intense that you close your eyes and enjoy the warmth. I suddenly felt a pain in my breast. As I opened my eyes, I saw that Jane's dad had bitten off half my nipple. The pain was gone as quickly as it appeared, and I then left his house.

I returned to my mother's house in Paulsgrove. She wasn't home, but Brand was. I felt so out of it; I had a bath and kept staring into space, I could hear loud noises, and it felt like I was dying. My heart rate was crazy fast. What had he given me? I had never experienced anything like it. I was petrified; I stumbled to the bathroom and vomited everywhere. I stared in disbelief at this thick black tar that covered the toilet bowl. Oh shit, I was going to die.

I had to leave the house and walk to Cosham to be collected by a stranger for a shift in Chichester. Every person that walked past was a threat. I thought they were trying to kill me! I stood in Cosham shaking, hearing things, and listening to dark thoughts of my looming death. I have never been more terrified in my life. I was certain I would die, yet there I was, off to work - now that is a good work ethic indeed. When I arrived at the busy restaurant, it was sensory overload; how I managed to learn new processes and actually perform was a miracle. My eyes were like black holes, my body was not mine, and neither was my mind. I continued to work there for a few more days, and the feeling inside of me lasted forever. I have no words to describe the fear, loss, and pure madness inside my mind.

I stopped taking drugs. For the first time in forever, I stopped. I couldn't shake the darkness or the feelings I experienced. I just drank alcohol. I needed familiar surroundings, so I decided to visit my favourite snooker hall. I received a visit from Jane; she sat outside the snooker club in the night air, looking scared.

Jane turned to me and said, "My dad said to come and find you. He tried to shoot me, and he said you could explain why."

As I looked at my best friend since childhood, I felt ashamed, so I said nothing. Jane continued to tell me how her dad got his gun out and fired it at her; luckily, he missed, but she had no idea why he did it.

I knew why. It was because I had not gone round to their drug den since I lost half my nipple, which grew back over the years, so that's interesting. I suspected he was mad over my disappearance, and this did not bode well for Jane.

Jane was stuck living at his house, probably in danger each day, but luckily Jane was eventually saved. A few of her father's friends were obviously worried for her safety, too, so they kidnapped Jane and placed her in hiding for a few weeks. Jane moved away, and our friendship was from a distance. Years later, our paths would cross again, but for now, our lives were separated.

Over the next few years, I met a man, and I fell in love. My drinking and drug use still continued, but it was less than before. My connection to supernatural voices and beings was lost for a while; I hardly ever saw or heard spirits now. The only time I really focused on it was when others brought it up. I would still be asked for readings, and at times, I offered snippets of information as proof of the afterlife.

I moved on from the previous restaurant and started a job in retail, but my life was pretty sad. I was in love with a destructive man. We struggled for money, I drank a lot, and we scrounged around, usually unable to eat or to finance all our lifestyle choices. We moved from a flat to a shared house, then back to my mother's. Eventually, I fell out with my mother; I sold all her furniture and abandoned her flat, leaving just two chipmunks in her property.

My boyfriend was on the run from the police, so we escaped to Foxton in Cambridge to live with a previous employer of his. I hated the countryside; the lady we lived with was a super bitch. She bred Boxer dogs, and she was 100% crazy. I took on two cash in hand jobs working at pubs; I worked the day shift at one and then the evening at the other. I was earning seven pounds an hour, which wasn't bad really for 2004. The minimum wage was £4.85 if you were over twenty-two years of age, and I was not. I missed home, and every day I would check the train timetable; I fantasised about returning to Portsmouth. I argued with my boyfriend as he felt I was depressed and neurotic; he had isolated me from my family and friends.

I felt lost and empty, and the darkness was taking over me, so I returned to Paulsgrove, leaving him in Foxton. Luckily, he had telephoned my brother Elijah to warn him of my plans as I sat in my mother's abandoned, empty flat, waiting to die. The chipmunks were not even there to keep me company as a lady in Foxton had heard about them; she had driven to the flat to collect them.

My brother Elijah rescued me again; he whisked me away and moved me into his house in Portchester. I helped his partner Janine with household chores; I kept Janine company and spent my days there. I had known Janine since I was three years of age; Janine is Jane's mother, and we were neighbours when I lived in Portchester as a child. I still needed the drink, and I never remember Jane visiting her mum Janine back then. A few weeks later, my boyfriend returned from Foxton and moved in with us, sleeping on the lounge floor and planning for a new place to live. We had become good friends with my brother and his partner; it was nice to bond with my brother, drinking whiskey until the early hours of the morning.

I couldn't deny that I was depressed. I started suffering from anxiety and night terrors, I would be awake, but my body was paralysed. The doctors put me on a multitude of tablets and referred me to therapy about my childhood. An easy way out if you ask me: blame everything on childhood. I started to receive visions; they were similar to ones I had experienced before. The visions were not nice ones, and I was struggling to determine the difference between reality and visions. I was peeling potatoes at Janine's sink, and boom, I saw my partner about to strike me from behind, so I turned and screamed. As I glanced around the kitchen, with a knife in hand, the others stared back at me with confusion. These visions continued, always violent and always wrong. I would respond as I felt fit: I was finally going mad.

On Valentine's Day, we enjoyed a lovely steak meal, and the room was filled with a balloon arch. The table was decorated nicely by Janine, I was handed a box of chocolates by my partner, and I was most surprised. It was that night in 2004 that my boyfriend dropped to one knee, held out a ring and proposed to me. The whole act was caught on camera, but all I did was laugh and demand to know where he had found the money to buy a ring!

It wasn't long before my fiancé and I moved into a place in Copnor on Dudley Road; it was a one-bedroom house. The property was paid for by my social benefits and organised through one of his friends. With wood chip wallpaper and a brown bath, it was a dump. We didn't care, we needed our own space, and it could easily be decorated to look nice. I was not working; the doctors had deemed me unfit for work, and quite rightly too. My fiancé worked cash in hand when he could, scrapping cars and the odd painting job.

Our arguments increased; he was becoming tired of my endless depression and issues.

One December, my fiancé said to me, "I have arranged for you to spend a few days at your brothers."

This request was not a suggestion and more of an order. I was told that I was out of control. This made no sense to me as I was not acting any different to usual, but I packed a bag and left to spend time at my brother's. It was only a few days before Christmas when I received a text message from my fiancé, it offered no reason, but he was breaking up with me. I was so confused, and I did not understand.

The following day Janine heard from her friend that a young girl had gone missing. The girl was a beautiful fifteen-year-old; she sang like an angel. I had met her through combined dinner parties as the girl's mother was best friends with Janine. I did not know where the child had gone, and my suspicions never fell to my fiancé. I was still texting and calling him daily, we spoke, and I received mixed messages. My brother and I believed he was having a funny five minutes, and we would soon make up again. A fool I was, as it was obvious to most that I was kept in the dark about the reality of the situation. My brother drove me to my house in Copnor as I needed more clothes and belongings. I was locked out of my own house. What the hell was going on? I climbed over the small wall to see if a window was left open, and as I peeked through the net curtains, my heart sank. I could see a girl's clothes on my bed and a stranger's clothes thrown carelessly all over my floor!!!!

I broke down the front door and charged into the house. I felt sick. How could I be so blind? I could smell her perfume! A sweet and sickly smell invaded my nostrils; it was familiar, like a fragrance most teenagers wear. I scanned my flat and all my furniture, but all I took was my VHS tapes! I had collected my films on VHS for many years; I shoved them in black bags before we returned to Portchester. My mind was racing; we were engaged, she was just a child, and my fiancé was twenty-eight years of age, for God's sake!

I broke that day; my already fragile mind was broken.

As I walked back into my brother's house and plonked myself down on the sofa, the doorbell rang.

I opened the door. "Hello, Jane."

That same day, my best friend Jane returned to live at her mother's house in Portchester. With bags of clothes and a broken relationship behind her, our paths had crossed again.

On New Year's Day, I was arrested for breaking and entering; a police car had pulled up outside my brother's house. I was walking past the police car when I was arrested; a great way to start the year! The police wanted evidence that the house in Copnor was in my name, my landlord was out of the country, and I had no paperwork on me. They requested receipts for all the VHS tapes that I had taken. Were they for real? I was locked up in a cell for hours, treated like a criminal. Eventually, Janine came to rescue me. She explained about my mental health, and they let me go. I was given a date to provide evidence of my tenancy to the police by, which I did once my landlord returned to the country over a month later.

Janine and my brother couldn't possibly put up with two of us; they already had five others living in their three-bedroom house. Janine told Jane and me to get jobs, so I scanned the newspaper and called the first number that I read. I arranged an interview for a few days after, and I was offered the job immediately. So, my crazy ass was returning to work. My doctor said I was unstable and that I shouldn't be working, but I didn't care.

Jane and I started taking drugs and wanted to escape the prying eyes of her mother, so we went to see Dan. Dan is Janine's ex-husband and Jane's ex stepdad; he rented a three-bed house in Eastney. Dan was looking to sublet the property for his landlady, who lived in Greece; she had met Dan's daughter once before. Dan's actual daughter she had met was Mercedes, so we needed to convince her via telephone that Jane was Mercedes. The task wasn't easy, but we managed it. The only catch was one of the rooms was home to a girl named Tammy. Luckily, she was young, pretty, and loved drugs too.

Living at Eastney with Jane was like watching a car crash waiting to happen; we were destructive and gave no fucks. The few years that we lived there were violent, evil, despair and near-fatal.

I slept with a kitchen knife under my mattress on each side; I had a baseball bat by the front door. An axe hung on my wall, and I watched Buffy the Vampire Slayer over and over. I was in extreme pain internally, I worked, and I drank from the moment my eyes opened until they closed again. I started to vomit blood when I was without a drink for too long, there was blood in my stool, and my thirst knew no limits. I would shake like a washing machine when my alcohol levels dropped, I partied hard, and I was like a bull in a china shop - destructive.

At times I returned to my church, The Portsmouth Temple of Spiritualism. I was not really connected to my supernatural gifts, but I recall being able to tune in when I wanted to. I received a reading from a medium at the church.

She said, "The pain, they hear your pain."

I was so full of rage and anger that I had to numb my insides with Jack Daniels. I would drink any alcohol sitting on my kitchen side, and when at work, I would walk across to the pub and down six double whiskeys. I would vacate work and walk into over twenty or thirty pubs on my way home, drinking one or two drinks in all of them. At home, I could down a bottle of Jack Daniels in twenty minutes; I had optics in my lounge and pills were strewn everywhere. I sold pills, too, so the company I kept was not the good kind. Throughout the day, I functioned; at night-time, I partied and then late at night, I would break down. Terrorised by my mind and dark thoughts, I would find comfort in Mercedes. We would chat and drink until the early hours of the morning, we became close, and a beautiful friendship was formed.

Jane started working with me for a month or so, but her head was troubled, and she soon left for a community carer job. Jane had a boyfriend in prison; he was a smackhead and who she would visit often. Jane could never keep up with my drinking or antics, so she took a new path – prescription drugs. Jane wanted peace and quiet, which is not something she would find here; I often spent nights with my axe raging to kill. I cannot blame Jane for eventually moving out; our friendship was no longer on the same path.

One evening after a night out, we argued. I used Jane's boot to hit myself in the head before throwing a remote at her. While I was lying in my bed, Jane walked in, holding a knife with blood pouring down her hands. Jane had cut up her own stomach.

She was mumbling, "The only person who had never hurt me in my life was you - until now."

Jane soon moved out while I was at work. A new girl replaced her quickly, but she was pregnant. How that poor pregnant girl put up with living with me is beyond me. Tammy had moved out too. A weird man moved into her room, but he did a bunk without paying his rent. Everyone was replaced; they would move in and then move out. I was the obvious reason; no one could even bear to live with me.

My drug use came to a head when I suffered a suspected heart attack. I was treated at Queen Alexandra hospital, where they placed me on beta blockers. I stopped drugs for one whole week!

I then returned to taking pills and adding in a heart tablet, but it did not work. I still passed out on the odd occasion. I often jumped in the bath to re-ignite my ecstasy fuelled buzz when having a party at mine. I fell a few times in the bathroom when I was off my nut on pills. On one occasion, I hit my head and fell back into the bathtub, and my eyes were wide open. My good friend screamed as I lay naked but was unresponsive. I came around, then fell again when I tried stepping out of the bath. Each time I popped a beta blocker pill in my mouth, I had no idea whether I would make it or not. I did not care; the risk was worth taking.

It was a family issue that finally led me to seek help for my addictions. My sister Vikki had pre-eclampsia, she was taken into hospital, and we were sadly told she might die. The doctors had no clue what was happening, and they kept moving her from ICU in Queen Alexandra hospital to another hospital called St Mary's. The chance of the baby surviving was low, as was my sister's chance of living.

It was at St Mary's hospital that my sister announced, "If I die, I want Bryony to raise my kids."

Trust me; I was the last person anyone wanted to raise their kids. Vikki had three children - Trae, Kayleigh, and Danni. I was gobsmacked, but after some thought, I concluded it would never happen. My drinking had taken a toll on my body and mind, and my speech was coming out backwards. As a control freak, I hated this, and I was less than pleased when the blackouts started too.

I rocked up to work at the call centre, hating my life and hating myself.

I started shouting on the calling floor, "I hate Mondays. No one likes Mondays!"

I cannot recall who it was, but someone turned to me and said, "Bryony, it's Friday." What the actual fuck? I had blacked out for five days! I had not one recollection of who I had seen or where I had been.

I left work and walked straight to Kingsway House, and they booked me in for an assessment. After my assessment, it was clear I needed help, so it was arranged that I would enter Nelson Clinic behind St James' hospital for rehab in two weeks' time. I was about to embark on my slow journey back to spirituality ....

Chapter 6

The thought of walking through the rehab clinic's door was looming over me; I had no idea what was awaiting me in the land of the sober. I was twenty-one years of age; it was now 2005, and I had been drunk since 1999! I sat on my bed drinking bottle after bottle of vodka. It felt like a wake, a goodbye, and farewell to the love of my life – shant. Never again would I say, "Wanna get a shant?" It was deeply sad, and I was not ready for what was waiting ahead.

Jane drove me to Nelson Clinic in Portsmouth, which was behind St James' Mental Hospital. Ironically, the building next door was a social club; how tempting and cruel. After answering many questions, I just wanted to sleep. I was allocated a bed in the corner of a room, but to sleep, I was not. The clinic didn't allow daytime sleeping, but the opportunity for group therapy and a communal lounge. I swallowed some much-appreciated tablets and glanced around the room. I was playing spot the addiction: smack, alcohol, smack, cocaine. It was easy to see what other people's poisons were. There was this one young lad who looked normal; he even had some weight on him.

I was referred to rehab for six weeks; at least four of them would be sleeping and living in the clinic, and possibly night release rehab for the remaining two weeks. We were not allowed alcohol-based mouthwash or even wine gum sweets as they had names of alcohol on them! There was this scary, tall lady with wide eyes and crazy big hair. I smelt her before I saw her, a vile stench of mouldy cabbage; she must have something rotting on her body. Let's name her Scary Mary. She had this expression on her face like she had seen a headless monster, and she smelt like death too. She looked like she should be in St James' hospital, as no birds flew over her cuckoo nest! I enquired as to her addiction, expecting the answer to be pain medication, but she was an alcoholic and worked as a nurse! A NURSE ...! She looked like she needed a nurse, that's for sure. I hope to God that Nurse Scary Mary is never treating me for any injury; she is more likely to play doctor with a scalpel than heal anyone!

I couldn't help staring at this toothless girl with enough grease on her hair to fill a wash bucket. The girl looked like shit and spoke like a drunken child. With scabs on her face and dark black eyes, she was the kind of person you crossed the street to avoid. I correctly pinned her as a smackhead, and she was flirting with the men in the room like a thirsty whore.

I spotted a group that I felt comfortable with, all red-faced and with waxy wrinkly skin was my kind of crowd. I was not accepted by the old alcoholics at first. I smelt different, and by different, I mean clean. I also had many teeth and a youthful face, so what could I possibly be doing in a place like this? The leader of the group studied me; his beady eyes inspected my appearance before questioning me.

"What do you drink, and how much? I drink up to eight cans a day."

Wow, wow, wow ... Steady on, Grandpa! I had previously been challenged many times before, and I had never lost; there was no way I was about to lose now. I informed him and his sheep that I drank half a bottle of vodka before work, several whiskeys during work and a few litres of whiskey in the evening. DROP THE MIC ...

Mr Beady nodded his head in approval; I had been accepted.

My first few days in rehab were pretty light; I was not given any chores to do yet. I spent my first morning moving pictures and furniture before the others woke up. I then sat back to watch as the confusion and questions invaded others' minds. You would not believe the arguments it can cause to move even one picture; most of their day consisted of them sitting staring at walls and studying the room.

The DTs set in - that means alcohol withdrawal symptoms for anyone who doesn't know. I needed a drink, and I needed it now, so I telephoned Jane. I explained that I needed some weed to settle my nerves, but Jane would need to pretend to be dropping off pyjamas. The plan was foolproof. As Jane turned up in the reception area, I was called to attend. I spotted Jane; thank God, I was saved! I was not so thrilled when the volunteer hatchet face decided to supervise my interaction, and Jane sheepishly handed me a size 8 G-string. I looked at Jane with daggers in my eyes, I was a size 12 waist at the time, and a G-string was not pyjamas. Hatchet Face eyed me suspiciously, and Jane started to cry; she said she needed to be near me and missed me. I hugged Jane tightly, and the Hatchet Face volunteer offered that Jane and I could walk around the garden edge. Thank the heavens above; there is a God. I walked around the hedges smoking my weed with Jane, laughing, and scolding her about the stupid G-string.

As I headed back inside, I felt clever, like I had outsmarted the system. Some people in rehab are referred by a doctor or an assessment centre, but some are ordered by court judges.

I hated the sweet sickly smell. If you have never experienced it in a toilet, then good for you. When a person urinates and they've been on certain drugs, their urine can be a sickly fragrance. This skanky lady was in the toilet next to me.

She then shouted under the stall, "Can I buy your piss?"

It then occurred to me that some people here are being urine tested, and I had no idea whether my name was on that list.

My first group therapy was interesting. I listened as Miss Toothless shared her background story, and I sympathised with her. I always felt I was above the heroin addicts and crackheads, but after hearing why she took it ... wow, just wow. This poor toothless woman had been raped repeatedly as a child, and she was then sold to a paedophile ring at age nine. As a child, she was used for many sick fantasies, and as she got older, she was drugged and hooked on heroin. Whenever she fell pregnant, the babies were taken from her and sold off to God knows where. I believe I would never take heroin or smoke crack, but my God, she was forced to, and who would ever want to be sober after that?

The young, chubby lad who wore a gold bracelet was also a smackhead; he had some teeth and was only in his early twenties or late teens. I will name him Chubs because he was pretty fat for an addict. Mr Chubs was from Gosport, what a shock, and he actually had a lot of money. Chubs was very open about the fact his childhood was great. He had money, so therefore, he didn't thieve like some addicts. In conclusion, Chubs blamed his problem on boredom. He wore the best clothes, and I am pretty sure he bathed too. My mindset was changing after hearing some of their histories and choices that got them to where they were.

I made friends with a new girl, she was slightly older than me, but as soon as she saw me, I became a target for her. Rehab was a room filled with mainly toothless, smelly, and older people. This group of misfits admitted they were sad, lonely drinkers or homeless and that they were even criminals at times. The new girl was pretty, blonde, and around twenty-six years of age; she liked to party! I will name her Miss White, for she was a cocaine addict, a schoolteacher and a functioning druggy. It was like being on another planet in rehab; the outside world was like a dream. It was not long before that dream came crashing into our planet. While we were sitting outside on the grass, enjoying the sunshine on our skin, a group of school children walked past. There was a public footpath that stretched past the rehab clinic and mental hospital. What the hell? I had never seen a pregnant woman move so fast. Oh, did I forget to mention that Miss White was six months pregnant? Reality invaded our planet like a sword in the throat, sharp and lethal.

I was soon allowed to visit the local store with other inmates in a group of four, and we had to walk past a pub to get into the local shop. That day I purchased some sweets, which were later confiscated as they had names of alcohol on them. When my four weeks were up, I was on tablets for the withdrawal symptoms to help with the shakes and hallucinations, plus vitamin B. Finally, I was allowed back home overnight; it was heaven to sleep in my own bed. I stayed off the drink and returned to the clinic daily. I formed a strange bond with the people I was in rehab with. I guess because we experienced a crazy time together. There was a sense of being united on that front, plus we shared dark memories and experiences with each other.

However, there is always one bad piece of fruit that upsets the apple cart, and I will name him Mr Big Stuff. It is shocking how fragile a person's recovery can be; one wrong move and BOOM, they are off the wagon. When Mr Big Stuff walked into Nelson Clinic, the wind changed. He was around 5'6" with short, curly black hair, and as I glanced over him, I knew he would be trouble. The gold medal goes to ... Bryony Best, for she is a fucking genius. Mr BS strutted in like he owned the joint; the slutty group of spice meths were on him like white on rice. He bounced as he walked, like that cartoon tiger named Tigger, and with a whore on each arm, he moved around the room like a bad smell. It is not surprising to know that he was there by court order, he looked stoned, and he was definitely packing. Meth whores are like flies, and where there are flies, there is certainly shit.

Mr BS had drugs on him; he floated to each group in the room. Like a pit bull wanting to fight, he'd just stare, waiting for a reaction so he could cause a scene. Interestingly enough, he never did come near me, we only caught each other's eyes once or twice, but he knew. The head of my group and the sheep was Mr Beady, and he instantly disliked Mr BS. After many arguments and lots of rolled cigarettes, Mr Beady threw the towel in, packed his belongings, and left. It was only a week until Mr Beady's sentence was up, but the apple cart had been upset, and so had he.

I heard a few days later that Mr Beady was back on the drink. He had previously fallen off the wagon after years of sobriety when a doctor had suggested that Mr Beady drink a glass of red wine each evening to help with his heart condition. Clearly, this advice was given without reading any background history. The single glass of red wine was enough to turn Mr Beady back to being dependent on alcohol, and this is what led him to rehab again in 2005.

My sister Vikki was starting to recover slowly, and she gave birth to a baby boy named Tru. Kayleigh had to nurse the baby from home as Vikki spent the next few months in hospital recovering.

Once I was released from Nelson Clinic, I decided that drinking wine wasn't really drinking as it has such a low percentage of alcohol, but I then received some bad news.

It was July 2005, and I had just bought myself a new pedigree Staffordshire Bullterrier. The dog was a reward to me for not drinking, not any real alcohol anyway. I named him Metz after the drink. I didn't drink Metz myself, though, as it was only for pussies.

My recovery was slow as I was still drinking in the evenings, but I had managed to stop drinking in the daytime. I had written letters to people to apologise for some of my behaviour; I never posted them, though. In my mind, I was sober; I hardly drank at all now, really.

I was visiting my sister Vikki at her place when there was a knock at the door. As I sat playing with my new dog, a bundle of joy in my arms, I felt loved. My brother Elijah and his partner Janine had arrived. After much whispering in the kitchen, I was invited for a drive. As I climbed into the back seat of their car, I noticed that Brand, my brother, was just sitting there, quiet. I remember thinking, 'Why is he here? Shouldn't he be at work?'

As we moved along the motorway, I focused on Metz. I could sense something was wrong; Brand didn't even look at my new dog. Janine was sitting in the front passenger seat; she turned to me and started to speak. I could hear what Janine was saying, but it was like I was underwater, and the noise from the motorway was like an increasing din.

My father was dead. My sister Trina had placed an advert in the paper looking for me and Brand. Janine and Elijah had responded to the advert, and that is how they discovered the news. I had not seen my father in many years; the police had been involved after an incident that took place between us, preventing him from contacting me. I had recently spoken with Jane since my heart issue fiasco, deciding that I would soon get back in contact with my father. A near-death experience can change one's outlook in life, changing their beliefs on what actions or situations they deem to be forgivable or not. I focused on my Metz; we were driving to Fareham to tell my mother the news. There we stood in the middle of the street, my mother, Brand and I, hugging.

The following day, I woke up and dressed for work like any other day. As I sat in the loud call centre with the buzz and chatter around me, I zoned out. Inside my head, I was spinning, repeating the words over like a mantra ... 'Your dad is dead ... Your dad is dead ... Your dad is dead ...'

It wasn't long before my manager could tell something was adrift. After spilling the beans about my father, I was sent home.

I walked straight into the pub; hello, darkness, my old friend.

I also had a story sold about me to Pick Me Up Magazine, a happy ending one about my rehab journey and me getting sober for my sister and her kids. By the time the story was printed, I was already out partying in the pubs and clubs again. Strangers would walk up to me in a club and say well done on giving up the drink. I would stand there with a Jack Daniels in my hand and thank them for their support. It was hilarious to me, but I also understood that I always looked sober to them.

A new kind of torment had walked into my life; I, of course, was the orchestrator of it all. I had fallen out with my brothers, Brand and Elijah. You make a few threats, buy a new gun, and suddenly you are a bad person. To be fair, I was a nutter, and my new obsession was Janine. Janine and my brother Elijah had drifted from me, but they had stayed friends with the ex-fiancé, you know, the one who now preferred under-aged girls. I would receive vile texts and calls from the ex and his new child, and I discovered that two little dickie birds were whispering my secrets of despair to them. This was a traitorous and unforgivable action, and it did not help that I knew Janine had stood as a character reference for my ex on a particular occasion. Add in the fact that Janine had known prior to my breakup that said ex had disappeared one night with the child in question, and what do you get? A cunt. Yes, Janine was a complete and utter cunt! I was like a dog with a bone, and all my fantasies involved killing three people: the ex, the child, and Janine. I still tolerated Janine, for she was my best friend's mother, and she was engaged to my brother.

The cat amongst the pigeons was my dog, Metz, as that super bitch stole him from me. Well, she didn't exactly thieve him; I gave him to my brother and Janine one day. It is important to remember that my father had just died, and I was not long out of rehab. I happened to be at Janine and Elijah's house with my dog Metz when my landlord informed me of the NO PET policy. I was distraught and confused, and the only solution at the time was for someone else to take the dog. With a wedding soon approaching, I bargained that the dog could be a wedding gift. The dog was beautiful and cost hundreds of pounds, so I suggested that my brother and Janine still pay me half the money that the dog had cost. I was booked on a plane to Ireland the following day to visit my father's gravestone, so my problem-solving skills were not at my strongest.

The following day, when I returned from Ireland, my sister Vikki offered me a fantastic solution, I could keep Metz at her house! I would still get to see him daily as we lived nearby, and I could train him and walk him. I excitedly telephoned my brother's landline, but there was no answer as they were out camping. I could hardly contain my joy over the idea of getting Metz back. I was sober-ish in life, my dad had just died, and I needed Metz.

Janine, however, did not find my news thrilling. In fact, she said, "He is our dog now." When I said I would take him back, she responded like a baddie from a film.

"I'd like to see you try!"

Challenge accepted. From that day forward, Janine was public enemy number one to me. My alcohol consumption increased back to its normal level, and I became out of control again. It was the catalyst for many family relationships breaking down, which only added to my fury as I blamed Janine for it all. So, in only a few short years, I had fallen out with my mother, and I had driven my best friend Jane to move out and abandon me. I burnt my bridges with Janine, and my brother Brand and Elijah were no longer speaking to me. I was obviously not invited to the wedding, and I had turned so hell-bent on vengeance that I planned to shoot my best friend and Metz just to spite Janine.

I feel it is safe to say that my life sucked until, one day, I received a cassette through my door. It read on the envelope – *To know where you're going, you have to know where you've been.* I recognised the writing immediately; it was Brands. I eagerly played the cassette; it was recordings we had done when we were younger, with Brand playing his guitar. I felt this was an olive branch or at least a ray of hope, so I sent Janine a letter. Janine must have taken pity on my letter, and she convinced my brothers to start speaking to me again. This was the first step back to normality.

The day had come when I was to move out of my drug drenched party den and really try to get sober. It was my good friend Cleigha who collected my sorry ass and dropped me off at my sister Vikki's house. I would be living at my sister's for a while until my new room was ready; my brother Brand had offered me salvation. Brand had just purchased a new house with his partner; he had invited me over to his studio flat for dinner to announce the news. I think Brand thought he could keep an eye on me there in a brotherly way. I was not taking many drugs anymore, and my drinking was still daily, but I kept it to the evening time and weekends.

I was overjoyed to be living with Brand again. As children, we fought loads, but we were very similar in most ways. I had a gorgeous bedroom in the new house, with wood flooring and a wall-to-wall mirrored wardrobe; it was wonderful. I was still working at the call centre, surrounded by a lot of bad influences, but I soon decided to step up and be present. I sat at my desk, surrounded by the smoke of despair, and I knew something had to change. I emailed my friend Mercedes with my CV, and that CV was put forward for an employment coaching job. I was a qualified trainer who had run restaurants and trained many staff members, and I was done with my take-a-break job. That is what I called my role at the call centre, a take-a-break job, as it is exactly what it says on the tin. I was a top salesperson in a very large company, but I didn't even need to try as it was effortless for me. It was time to pull up my big girl pants and get a challenging job.

Moving in with Brand in 2006 and then finally, in 2007, getting into a new job was just what I needed. I stopped taking drugs, except Valium, but they didn't count. In 2007 when I started my new job, I could not turn up smelling of drink or high on drugs, yet at the call centre, it was weird if you didn't turn up that way. My new job was important; I was back teaching and training others which I love doing. Brand was a great influence on me, too, he went to the gym every day, and I invested in a cross trainer.

This was the big turning point for me, a new start and, a year or so later, a new job. I welcomed the changes around me, even if it didn't look that way on the outside. I was becoming increasingly obsessive about being in control. I liked to control everything, and my ticks were getting more apparent. I would count numbers and tap my fingers and head as a coping mechanism. Brand's partner didn't help, though, as her English was not great, so she often just called me fat in a very direct way, but it did encourage me to exercise.

As I drank less and less, I became more anxious. I worried that people outside might be after me. I would see these gold stars in the corners of my eye; I spent a whole evening looking at the moon as I could see a face on it. I was trying to live sober, but it was hard. I was training on my cross trainer daily after work. I walked to work, and after 2007, I stopped day drinking 100%. The world is a hard place to be; emotions and feelings were infecting me like a disease. Unstoppable and intent on taking me as its victim, I should have fought back, but my strength evaded me.

Family bridges were starting to be rebuilt, but the hate and venom for Janine were still hiding inside of me like a cancer. I had taken some big steps in my recovery, but I was not perfect; I was still drinking most weekends and taking Valium in the evenings. I needed to take the tablets to chill my mind out; sometimes, I found reading a book would quieten the voices in my head. I walked half in the real world and half in another; I experienced voices and extreme cases of paranoia. During my recovery, I would vomit daily and multiple times. I would shake like a crazy person and see and hear things. I felt others were out to get me; my stomach would be in knots. I tried to relieve this hell by exercising, which helped; I also started meditating with a CD that was for anxiety. My doctor felt all of this was because I was now sober and not taking drugs. I could function normally one minute, and then, in the next breath, I was like a mad person. What was wrong with me, as this was pure hell?

I started to attend The Portsmouth Temple of Spiritualism for healing, it helped, but it was no cure. I even accused people of trying to kill me by poisoning my body moisturiser! I had no understanding of this physical and mental torment I was going through, so I kept thinking it was caused by others.

I was seen by a therapist, and when I said how I feel is not normal, he responded with, "What would you know of normal when you have been drunk for years?"

He had a point, so was I to believe that all drug addicts and alcoholics feel this way?

I thought I had been doing so well, but how wrong I was. I believed I had already been through hell in my life, but what was to come next was truly my darkest hour ...

Chapter 7

The darkest period of my life has to be the time between working at the call centre and moving in with Brand. When I first started to live my life more sober than drunk, I experienced the most outrageous things. For over two years, I lived in hell; I tried everything in my power to overcome the demons, but with no joy.

To backtrack slightly, I was released from rehab, I reduced my drinking greatly, and I even attended AA. Alcoholics Anonymous was a funny place, and I mean that literally. NA, which is Narcotics Anonymous, was full of paranoid nut jobs and freaks of the variety kind. When I first walked miles to AA, situated in a large room in Lake Road, Portsmouth, I was 100% sober. I think it was my first week out of rehab. Jane had offered to come with me, which sounds supportive, but not when she made me wait outside Elly Wines like a dog. Jane walked out happy with a few beers to down before attending AA; she stank of shant and sounded drunk too. As we approached the large hall, I recalled attending there for my niece's birthday party years earlier. I snuck out with Nadine to buy cigarettes; now, she was a cool cat.

There must have been around thirty-plus alcoholics in the room, including a nice-looking lad who smiled at us. Jane soon sat next to him, working her magic. The men and women were so friendly, we were a mixture of ages, and some were only binge drinkers. As Jane said hello to others, I spotted their noses twitching as the penny dropped; many clicked on that she had been drinking. Anyone with eyes could have spotted us earlier standing at the end of the gravel path while Jane drained her last can. I felt slightly embarrassed; this was a new emotion for me. I don't think Jane realised just how rude or dangerous it was to turn up drunk to an AA meeting. The whiff of beer was like placing a plate of steaming hot bacon under a weight watcher's nose: cruel and tempting.

As we sat in a very large circle, others started to share their stories of when they hit rock bottom. One guy reminisced about telephoning another AA member to borrow a bottle opener shouting, "Well, you won't be using it!" A rather large man in his early twenties shared a more serious tale; he was explaining how he was so low that he slit his wrists for attention. In his mind, a poetic scene would unfold, as a friend would telephone for an ambulance while saving him from death. He sent the room into a fit of awkward laughter when his rock bottom was realising he didn't actually have any friends, so he needed to telephone the ambulance himself. With a thumping heart, I walked to the front of the stage and collected my round silver chip; the chip read 24 hours on it. We then chanted the serenity prayer while holding hands, and I felt part of the group. I never did go back to AA as I only lasted a few more days of being truly sober, and my first chip of sobriety was also my last.

In all honesty, after rehab in 2005, I was drinking off and on and having a few sober days and a few sober nights. I moved house to live with Vikki, and then I was invited to live with Brand. I was working at the call centre, and I stopped buying or selling drugs. It was then within this transitional stage that my doctors shrugged off all my weird symptoms as alcohol and drug withdrawal. Eventually, I did get a new job, and I started my new role as a trainer and coach. However, before that new role started, I was very dark on my colour chart. For argument's sake, let's say that when my addictions were at their worst, I was *noire*, and by the time I had my heart scare and near-death experiences, I was dark brown as my drug intake reduced. When I moved to Vikki's house, I was a deep purple as I was just drinking, and then as I started living with Brand in Southsea, I was a slightly lighter shade of purple. Others may see just an alcoholic or a drug addict, but the levels or stages are very different. It is not fair to say that I was the same, as my intake and mindset were forever changing. I was accepting medical intervention and therapy too. I would love to say that I found the strength, and BOOM, I was cured, but recovery for me was slow and hard.

While living with Brand and working at the call centre, I had the most challenging time of my life. It was the transitioning stages that broke me; I remember explaining to doctors that I could see dots all the time. I felt people were after me, and at times, I didn't want to leave the house. My heart pounded, and I could hear voices and see things. One night I recall closing my eyes and seeing pictures. I was transported to a river so black in colour. I knew there was a body in the water, a murder victim, maybe? I could feel her pain and sense her presence with me. I then heard a voice as clear as day shout, "KILL YOURSELF." It was not my voice, yet it was coming from inside my room. I switched on my bedroom light and started to read a book. I found books helped when my mind swirled out of control.

I started to hear more voices like this as my life started to change, I would often begin to shake, and my adrenaline was always at full speed. My cross trainer helped with this, but it was only temporary. I opened up to a few doctors, but all they saw was a drug addict and alcoholic; none of them tried to really help. My health, while I was drinking, was okay, my stools usually had blood in them, and I sometimes vomited blood, but then again, I did have a history of stomach ulcers. When I reduced my alcohol, my body started to break, and I suffered from water infections constantly! Eventually, after a few years of UTIs and pains, I was diagnosed with Interstitial Cystitis. My stomach hurt most days, and I was treated for stomach ulcers. I still suffer from this condition to this day.

I was sixteen when I first had a stomach ulcer, so it's not surprising I still suffer from this pain. I felt dizzy and sick every single day. As I walked, the floor moved, and my body often had a sinking feeling. Could you imagine having to walk to work with the ground moving like the sea, feeling dizzy and sick and being sober? Now let's add in a few stomach pains, usually from regular gut rot and a water infection! The icing on the cake was my body shaking like a washing machine while hearing voices and wondering who was going to attack me from behind. This was my life without drink - not to mention fucking boring. I begged the doctors to help, and all they said was these symptoms would not last for very long. Oh, not forgetting the little chestnut statement from an unsympathetic doctor, "Most people find this happens when they give up the drink." They were completely wrong as those symptoms, as they called them, lasted for YEARS! Yes, bloody years.

I felt I was going completely insane. I did find a CD that helped me, it was one that supported anxiety, and it really helped me with my meditation skills. I meditated several times a day between the madness and voices. My sanity was pushed to its limits if I travelled abroad, a place I still fear to this day. Most people love a holiday, but oh no, not me.

I had my first mental breakdown in Bulgaria; it was back in the days when I was still drinking in the evenings and on weekends. I planned a holiday with my best mate, Casey, and it was one I will never forget. I lived with Brand, but I still worked with Casey at the call centre, so it must have been 2006. I was blonde then, with shoulder-length hair and big boobs. Casey was vertically challenged and had short blonde hair, too; poison dwarf was her nickname! She had led an interesting life, and we had become best friends; she loved a shant and was not shy around men, either. Together we were crazy. When we walked into a party, it was doomed to end in either a fight or a fuck. We didn't care much which one it was; all we wanted was to drink, dance and fuck men. Casey was a great friend to me; we had some bloody good nights, show-stopping weekends and epic parties.

We connected on a different level; she had a rough upbringing, and so did I. We were both thirsty for escapism and not afraid to fuck or fight anyone and everyone. With a mouth like a sailor and the hunger for fun like a clown, we travelled all over Portsmouth, wreaking havoc everywhere we went. I could fit Casey in my coat pocket, but when it kicked off … she would fight like a street gang member. Separate, we were fierce, but together, we were unstoppable.

We partied and visited pubs on holiday, as most people do; we slept with random strangers and danced away our blues. While getting dolled up for a night out, I felt unusual, and I started to shake. I felt paranoid, like others were waiting to kill me once I stepped outside the room. Casey brought me some food, and I couldn't even drink alcohol; I was so mentally unstable. I decided that I felt the way I did because I had been drugged. I pinned it all on a barman, blaming him for my newfound madness. I was scared as I lay in bed hearing voices while watching Buffy the Vampire Slayer in another language and a different country. The only way to explain it is to say I was going mad. I stopped drinking, and I was convinced that I would die. After that event, I always feared getting onto a plane. I assumed I would go mad in another country and be stuck in a foreign place as a nut case.

Over time, this anxiety about travel only increased. I recall standing on a train platform, crying in despair, on the telephone with Vikki because I was petrified about flying to France. I asked Vikki to book me an appointment for the day I returned with a doctor from St James,' as I felt this was the last straw. I couldn't take it anymore or lie to myself and others. I had to admit that even though I hardly drank and had considered myself sober for years, I had ultimately gone mad. As I stood at Southampton train station waiting at the airport to catch a plane to France, I had given up. I was about to visit my mum in France, and she would know I was not Bryony but an imposter instead. My relationship with my mother had transformed over the years; since my father's death, we had started to heal old wounds. It was a slow process, but we were learning to be mother and daughter again.

I bumbled through my trip with my mother. She knew something was wrong, and I broke down in tears. As she held me in her arms, I could smell her perfume, and I could hear her heartbeat. She was breaking, too; no mother wants to see their child in pain. As I returned to England, I had my appointment booked for a mental assessment. I felt a type of relief as I knew that soon, I would be helped by a professional.

When my assessment day arrived, I travelled to St James' alone. I signed into the reception book and was escorted to a small room. My doctor had referred me for a mental health assessment after my behaviour of shouting at strangers in the street had increased. My sister finally made me the appointment that I needed; I was scared to go. I answered all their questions as honestly as I could; they kept asking if the TV ever spoke to me or gave me orders. I sat alone, wringing my hands together, wondering what their verdict might be. The male doctor sat back down and handed me a leaflet, and he said I was suffering from psychosis. I had no idea what he meant. The leaflet stated facts about having superpowers, hearing voices, having visions and the bad effects of watching video games. Apparently, I was having breaks from reality and grand ideas of myself having superpowers. I enquired as to the treatment options, and he said tablets would suffice.

As tears weld up in my eyes, I asked my final question. "Will the tablets make me fat?"

The doctor replied, "Well, they can make people feel drowsy or less motivated to partake in exercise."

Hmmmmm, nope! No way was I taking tablets and getting fat. I refused their medication and left. As I floated away from their room and their scary diagnosis, I pondered my future. I could be sane and fat or slim and insane. Well, I chose the last option, so I must have been mental!

I soon received a new appointment. After visiting my GP, I was informed it was likely I would be sectioned. FINALLY...! No more bills or work. I could sit in a white room and take Valium all day. First,

I would be required to attend a final appointment at Cavendish House, and then I would be the star of Bryony Flew over the Cuckoo Nest.

I telephoned my sister Vikki. I cried tears of sadness, and I whimpered down the phone. The only silver lining was that Vikki's partner Liam worked at St James' Hospital. As a security guard, Liam walked the grounds protecting the outside world from any patients that might escape and stopping any released early mad ones from breaking back in!

My mind was racing, and so was my heart, as I sat in front of another doctor, spilling all my secrets and my astonishing life. I had spoken with many before, and that included therapists. One lady refused to help me as I smiled at her confused face.

The lady therapist asked me, "Why are you smiling?"

She didn't even blink as she stared at me, perplexed. After hearing my horrific life story, she was astounded that I was functioning to the level I was. She said she could not help me and sent me away, turning down money and a possible long-term patient. So, there I sat, planning my new appearance of being fat and crazy; a room with a view was all I would ask for.

That day, the doctor did not jump to the usual conclusions as many had before.

He simply said, "You are dangerously overconfident, and you have a God complex. I do not understand or agree with this spiritualism thing, but I suggest we try developing that skill instead."

And others thought I was the mad one! I had already explained that there was no way that all these dark and twisted voices were spiritual.

I spoke about my dealings with spiritualism and how warm and nice it felt. Yet this doctor wanted to waste time developing my gift as he believed it might help. How can madness be caused or cured by that? TWAT!

Being sectioned was inevitable to me, but I went through the motions, and I signed up and paid for a development course with the Portsmouth Temple of Spiritualism. I thought it would be a waste of time and a waste of money; what a crock of shit to drag this all out in this way. The church development circle gathered on a Friday evening at 7 pm. I did love the church as I liked the atmosphere and energy of the building too. I was well known at the church, for I had attended services there for years. I preferred it to the spiritual church in Fratton. It was also handy that I lived less than twenty houses down the road – a short walk, and I had arrived.

As I let the room wash over me, I couldn't help but think back to my pleas in that very same room. I lost count of the many times I sat in the audience, shouting to the spirit world in my mind.

"Just tell me it's you, and I will be okay. Please, God, help me. Dad ... Grandad ... Dot ... ANYONE... Tell me the voices are the spirit world, so I know I am not just mad."

No one ever responded, and no messages ever came through from any of the mediums on the platform. As I sat in the church in pain and with my mind in turmoil, I was never eased of my fears, and no answers were given. That is how I knew without a shadow of a doubt; that the voices in my mind were not messages from any spirits.

The first few sessions were very basic; we learned how to meditate and clear out our minds, ready to receive messages. I very much enjoyed this process: we grounded ourselves and opened our chakras, raising our vibration higher to communicate with the spirit world. I was taught about energy and how to prepare myself to be more open to receiving spiritual guidance and messages. We did not give readings as this group was for beginners; it was more of an introduction to mediumship. One lesson consisted of learning how to be an instrument for spiritual healing; I was interested and excited about this as I was definitely in need. After our usual meditation, grounding and lifting our vibration, we channelled healing energy. I spoke with my guides and discussed what the objectives were; I felt the tingling vibration as a light shone down through my crown chakra, along my arms and out of my hands! It was joyful, and I was triumphant. I basked in glory as I was able to do it with ease.

Another week we were placed into pairs, and after cleansing our chakras with visualisation and opening up our auras, we held out our hands and closed our eyes. Slowly walking towards each other, we were searching for a feeling of pressure or heat against our palms. It was amazing. I could literally feel another person's aura. It was not solid like a corporeal object, but if you followed all the steps correctly, you could feel, manipulate and throw energy! This was fabulous; I was taking to it like a duck to water. Many others struggled with learning the new skills and tasks, but I found it all so familiar.

When we would meditate, a share session would begin. As a learner, I still had naughty thoughts invading my meditations. It was through these experiences that an opportunity was made for me to ask a burning question.

"I have this friend, and she drinks sometimes and used to do drugs. When my friend drinks, she sometimes suffers for days, hearing bad voices. She is scared and thinks she is going mad."

The leader of the circle probed for more information, as she wanted to know more about these evil voices. I gave more knowledge about my "FRIEND" and eagerly waited for a response.

I was given a response from the spiritual development group leader in a metaphoric way that could easily be understood. Imagine if you had a house party and the front door was left open. The music is pumping, and strangers may think it sounded like fun was happening inside. The door being left open is an invitation to every Tom, Dick, and Harry! When a person who is sensitive to the supernatural drinks alcohol and takes drugs, they are not usually in control of themselves. They would shine bright like a party with a front door left open, attracting EARTHBOUND SPIRITS.

Wow, shut the front door, well, spiritually anyway. I was not convinced of this theory, but what did I have to lose?

If I could continuously stop drinking and learn to control my spiritual skills, I could ensure I wasn't always so open to unwanted lower energies. This certainly seemed attractive as it would stop the madness; all I had to do was to stop my occasional nights of drinking and learn to develop myself spiritually. So, I might not be mad, and my negative habits were making me a beacon for earthbound spirits that were not wanted. I was enrolled on a six-week course, and I had already completed two weeks, which gave me four more weeks to master this course and test this theory.

Challenge accepted ...

Chapter 8

As I lay my head down on my pillow, my mind spun with questions about the possibility of my future and mental health. On the one hand, it was a relief on some level to give in to the darkness, to be fitted up for a white jacket and a prescription pillbox. I wouldn't have to wash my hair or shave my legs! I have to be honest; the no-leg-shaving was a deal clincher for me; I was sold on that point alone. The belief that I was truly mad and losing my mind was lonely; I felt as if no one on this planet understood me. I could have been a cauliflower living amongst seals, which is how different I felt compared to others living in society. Most of my conversations happened either inside my head or with voices that no one else could hear. To be 100% crazy would have been easier, but to have some awareness and know you were falling down that rabbit hole was just cruel.

I started letting go of the vision I had in my mind, and I began to focus on the possibility of control: the ability to control my addictions and the voices. A light had been turned on inside of me, and I was planning on paying that bill.

As Friday approached, I walked into the Temple of Spiritualism like a boss. I had stopped swallowing Valium like they were Tic Tacs, and on Friday night, I was not drinking as I had a commitment to this development course. Most evenings began with meditation and grounding; after using visualisation to cleanse our auras, we would raise our vibration. The vibration on this plane is very slow and dense, which is why or how we have materialistic existence. The spirit world frequency is much faster; in order to try and communicate with spirit, we needed to raise our vibration. You can raise your vibration by talking about subjects from your higher self or crown chakra.

Before a service begins, when a medium performs on stage with a demonstration of mediumship, the audience usually sing to lift the energy and vibration in the room. We did not sing in my development group, but I did when I attended a demonstration. Guided meditation is when someone leads the direction of the meditation; time is allocated for non-facilitated visualisation too. I enjoyed the part of grounding oneself; I like connecting with the earth. You may recognise the more common tasks of this aim: when a person takes off their shoes and walks on the grass to ground themselves and to feel more centred.

At the start of my meditation, we would visualise to connect with the earth, before opening up our chakras and cleansing them with a waterfall or rainfall. There are many ways to achieve the desired outcome; this was followed by a process called "A Pack Away." I would create a room inside my mind, with windows left open to allow thoughts to come in and go as they please. Each meditation would require me to pack away my thoughts for the day into boxes. The less desirable boxes were thrown out the front, and the good boxes were stored out the back. I would visualise myself cleaning the room inside my mind. This process helps to put the day's events to the side, ready for the mediation.

The next step usually involved ascension of sorts; this could either be a direct route to the next level, or I could stop halfway up to the destination. On my pit stop, I could enter a beach or forest; it all depends on where we are asked to visualise. We are only given minimal advice and guidance on these meditations, leaving the blanks to be inserted by ourselves or intuition. The blanks are usually hidden in deeper meaning or offer insight into a situation or self-knowledge.

After the meditation was over, we would share our experiences with the group. Soon, we were asked to give advice to each other on what the hidden meanings could be. One gentleman named Tom said he kept being given an apple in his meditation, and the advice given was that he was learning new skills and being offered opportunities to grow. Another lady would see a pearl when she meditated, and one person felt this was because a message of wisdom was being offered. The people giving advice on the meanings of these symbols were speaking from intuition or their guidance.

As the weeks went by, the messages and explanations became more detailed. With trust in their hearts, people were sharing their thoughts, and they were correct. I was giving people messages as well as advising on their mediation's symbolic meanings and specific messages. For example, interpreting and explaining to someone that they had just lost their job and were feeling worried .... Others in the group were amazed at receiving such detailed and correct information. They were messages from our own mouths, but where was the knowledge coming from?

Most people just knew the information in an instant. For others, they heard their own voice inside their head, but they intuitively knew, like instinct, that it had come from somewhere else. I can only share my own experiences and knowledge with the world, but certain TV shows and films can mislead people into thinking that communicating with spirits is easy or smooth. I am sure there are a few mediums out there who can speak with spirits as easily as we can on the telephone, but they are few and far between.

Doris Stokes' books amazed me, as Doris Stokes did not even believe she was able to perform clairvoyance. Doris was messing around, pretending to be a fortune-teller as a joke, when others all confirmed that everything Doris said was correct! Doris was just saying any thoughts that came into her head; in shock and awe, the crowds of people around her were impressed. Doris then went on to live a life dedicated to working for the spirit world, including helping the police locate missing persons or bodies at times when called upon. Doris Stokes was born on January 6th, 1920, in Grantham and died on May 8th, 1987, as a spiritualist/self-proclaimed medium and author.

As for me, I received instant knowledge, and I also received answers to questions when I asked them inside my mind. When I saw spirits during my time in development, I usually felt a presence, and I could describe them from instant knowledge or visions from my third eye. It may be easier to understand if I rephrase it to 'my mind's eye.' If I said to you, "Picture a pair of red shoes in your mind," where do you see them? Are the red shoes inside your head, in front of your eyes or somewhere else?

If I close my eyes, I can see visions inside my mind, but if my eyes are open, I can see them in front of my eyes. I do not always see them as a solid corporeal form but more as a vision. Imagine you are in your lounge, and you want to move the furniture. You may look at different areas of the room, visualising various chairs or pictures in other positions. Your visions are not corporeal, but you use your mind's eye or visualisation.

I have seen corporeal spirits, and I have heard voices outside my head. Audio clairvoyance is how I describe a voice that I hear in the same way that I can hear another living person's voice on this earth plane when they speak.

The most important skill I wanted to master was controlling the ability to turn the voices off. Imagine my disappointment when I discovered that this was not an easy or possible skill. I was told that if I visualised myself getting into a box and closing the lid, I could stop the voices. At the time, I believed this information; therefore, I managed to manifest it into existence. However, as I was learning more skills and developing my abilities, more supernatural activities unfolded. I was nearing the end of my course when I realised that I was accomplished at it; I was naturally gifted. I did not struggle as others seemed to, and I believe it was my confidence and attitude that propelled me forward in this area. I was not hearing the dark voices and my paranoia was at an all-time low. Had that doctor been correct after all, and had Miss Development Leader been right too?

Only time would tell, and my forthcoming doctor review appointment was hanging over me like a sloth – heavy and lazy.

I opened my eyes and I looked around my room; it was pretty, and I loved my flooring. As it was an east-facing room, the sunshine danced through the window, caressing my skin. My appointment was half-eleven with Doctor Maybe: maybe he would section me but then again, maybe not.

As I walked toward Cavendish House on Victoria Road South, my heart was pumping, and my stomach felt like it had been tied in a knot by an expert seaman. I thought my little session would have been harder, but Doctor Maybe seemed very relaxed and welcoming of my news. I explained to him about my development group and that my dark voices and evil visions had decreased to zero, and BINGO! I had won a ticket to freedom!

It was disappointing that I did not witness a big red stamp of SANE on my paperwork, but hey-ho, I was not going to be committed, so all was good. With my new freedom came responsibility, for I needed to continue with this newfound spiritualism and stay on the wagon. The wagon was pretty; it was warm with lights and bells on its sides. I felt cold inside all the time, and the little voice in my head kept saying, "DRINK, BITCH, DRINK!"

One may assume that the idea of drinking and falling prey to lower energies and earthbound spirits, added to a side of crazy, would be enough to keep one scared into sobriety. Well, one would be wrong. As my cravings ran as deep as an ocean, I did not know how to live in this world sober. I had lived over half my life intoxicated, and taking off the rose-coloured glasses was both painful and shocking!

I was still working at the call centre after my diagnosis of being sane; however, my colleagues at the time would beg to differ. No one really knew what the new normal would look like, and neither did I. I would walk to work listening to music and taking in the sights and smells surrounding me. Once at work, I would focus on meeting my targets, which was never hard, really. On my lunch break, I would eat a sandwich and sit in the break room, rather than repeat my old habits of walking into the Fleet and Firkin for a few warm whiskeys.

I made friends with an Australian female named Sammy; she was like a broken bird that couldn't fly. She had these terrible mood swings that could knock a house over. She had a crystal on her desk, and at times, she would let others hold it. It never got warm, no matter what you did to it. Sammy was a spiritualist, too; we both were on a journey returning to spiritualism and desperately seeking a better life for ourselves. As I spent more time with Sammy, I could feel her pain; she was in torment. From my point of view, Sammy was in the end stage of a destructive phase of her life and probably battling her own demons. It is brave and courageous for anyone to live in a strange country and build a life for themselves. I have much admiration for people who are strong enough to leave their old life behind to start afresh.

I continued to attend the Temple of Spiritualism, and I invested in some Crystal Tarot Cards. I had never been drawn to any other type of cards except crystal ones. The pack that I had spotted years before in a lovely shop in Emsworth was perfect for me. The cards had pictures of crystals and elements on them, and the messages, if you read from the accompanying book, were higher messages of spiritual guidance. Every one of us here on earth is on a spiritual journey; we are learning lessons, and we have many paths to decide between. I was seeking my purpose, and the tarot cards matched my desires and outcomes. I was not interested in materialistic things and knowledge about my loved ones or career. The cards can produce this information when the reader uses mediumistic or energy reading tactics, but for a person reading from the book, all messages were of a life purpose nature.

Sammy and I would spend time together outside of work. I practised my card reading skills with Sammy, and vice versa too. When we would read for each other, we never turned the card over until the end, so the card would lay face down. I would hold my hand over the card and ask my spiritual guides for clues about the type of card that lay beneath my hand. For example, I may see fire in my mind's eye. If I turned the card over and it was a fire element, then I would be reassured of my abilities, and the trust between myself and my gifts would grow. As my hand hovered over the card and I gave Sammy a reading, I would be tuning into and focusing on Sammy's energy. As time progressed, I might feel a presence drawing near, and messages from spirit may come through. The mixture of aura and mediumistic readings were often detailed and correct, all the time strengthening my connection with spirit and my guides.

Sammy liked crystals, and we sometimes held amethyst or quartz crystals to heighten our experiences and connection. I found crystals fascinating but also daunting, as there were so many, and they have such different uses and components to memorise. I found great comfort in spiritualism, and each day I felt a little stronger. I did a daily card reading on myself, and when I did this, I would read the message from the crystal book rather than tap into other avenues of knowledge.

As time was slowly moving by, I began to change and grow. Don't get me wrong; I was not fixed by a long shot. I was getting on well living with Brand and his partner; I even started exercising more regularly. Sammy convinced me to attend a kickboxing class. It was violent and hard, but I was completely addicted to it. My first ever lesson was so exhilarating. We did stretches and breathing techniques, and then I was partnered up with the shortest girl in the group and instructed to do power kicks. I apologised as I looked at the small, terrified girl before blasting her with several kicks. I could hit people and not get arrested; this was heaven. I was sweating like an MP at a COVID party, but it was worth it. I was not the best in class, but I left there wanting to be. I made a pact with Sammy that we would train at my house to become kickboxing queens.

We kept our promises, and after work, twice a week at least, we stretched out our legs together, and we sparred. I bought some red hand and leg pads; it was awesome, and afterwards, I felt so calm and relieved. I never understood why the advice was given to people with anger issues to attend boxing or martial arts, but now I did. Mentally it was like taking a Valium; I felt chilled out, and my body was equally sore but tired too. It aided with my sleeping, and I felt strong. I practised more and more each day, getting faster and faster. I even started teaching my niece Danni and her friends too, and soon Kayleigh also wanted to learn how to fight properly. Most of us had experienced multiple street fights, but now we were powerful and precise with our hits. Mercedes' sister Shelly even joined us one evening for a spar session, and it was great. Shelly could do the splits, and she was a typical Pompey girl who was always fighting. She had more front than Brighton beach too. Shelly loved it, and we had a great time. We wore protective gear when we fought, so no one ever got seriously injured. I could always take a hit, but I also felt it was important not to be scared of getting punched. I would hold the pads and intentionally let new starters clip me slightly. The first time they made contact with a face was always funny as all they did was apologise.

I was forming healthier habits and new relationships, too; it was empowering to be in control. I do recall a close friend sitting on a bus and discussing my exercise habits with her. I was concerned as I was using my cross-trainer for longer and longer each day. I was mixing cardio with kickboxing, swimming and running. My friend Lizzy mentioned that the best thing to do would be to change the intensity of my workout rather than to exercise longer. Lizzy then turned to me and said, "You have an addictive personality, and you do everything until it breaks."

Lizzy's words echoed inside my head, and I have never forgotten them; neither have I ever heard another person sum up my approach to everything in life so correctly. In rehab, they talk about swapping one addiction for another; well, at least this new one was legal. My obsession with control stemmed and grew like a weed, relentless and unstoppable. I was curious about what other areas of my life were affecting my results and outcomes.

I decided that I would lose weight and eat lower fat and healthier food. I reduced my fat intake by 60%, and for some months, I would only eat cabbage or sweet corn. My favourite food was salmon and vegetables, this was a treat, but I still needed to exercise on certain foods to evaluate the outcome. I enjoyed being in control and watching my body and mind change. Unfortunately, my obsession subject moved towards humans. I wanted to know what would happen if I cut certain people out of my life? Periodically, I would stop talking and visiting XXX, and then a few weeks later, I would swap XXX for another XXX. It was fascinating to study the differences that my mind and life felt when I controlled who was interacting with me. These studies did take a darker path when I moved on to my new question: what power of influence did I have on others?

I played silly and childish games with colleagues at work, telling rumours to certain people and watching as the calling floor turned into a battlefield. I found it interesting how easily manipulated others were. I concluded that my personality demanded respect and that others wanted my approval. This is still similar to this day, but for different reasons. I did some unspeakable things, really, all in the name of research. None were illegal, and no one died, but they were still questionable tests I facilitated on others. This control issue soon spiralled away from me, and I became the victim of my own thoughts.

I never knew it at the time, but I was showing traits of OCD. Obsessive Compulsion Disorder is an easy issue to conceal. It can also easily go unnoticed, as many aspects can be misidentified as a person's quirks or personality traits to the untrained eye. At first, my family and friends thought it was funny to watch me freak out if they moved an ornament or item in my room. My silences were normal as I counted pavement slabs or steps in the street. As soon as my brain thought up a question, I needed to know the answer. It did not matter if that required me to start over and walk back home to count the bricks or if it meant brushing my teeth a certain number of times while counting in groups of five which I repeated over and over. I had always bounced my knee up and down when seated, so it was not a massive change when I started tapping my fingers while counting numbers inside my head.

My tick escalated when I was super stressed, and I would tap my head and visualise a set of numbers coming out of my head in sequences of 1, 2, 3, 4, 5. I would then tap a different area of my head, and a new set of numbers in the same sequence would flow out of my head but with a different timing from the first set. I also found that when I stood still, I felt sick from the ground moving beneath my feet, so I started to pace and rock back and forth in time to a beat and number frequency inside my head. From a stranger's perspective, I would look crazy, going full speed with all ticks simultaneously happening. However, inside I felt better; all the ticks or movements would bring me comfort or make me feel less sick.

I invented new processes to help me cope. For instance, when I felt overwhelmed, I would make lists inside my head of things that I needed to do. When I completed one of the items, it would turn green inside my head, where all items started off as a red light. Too many red lights were bad news, but the green lights made me feel better. This process was very helpful at first, but soon my daily vomiting, which started when I stopped drinking alcohol, had increased. When I had too many red lights inside my head, I would vomit more. I must sound absolutely barking mad, but my control issues extended to friends too. If Mercedes' house was untidy and messy, it would give me mental and physical pain. I couldn't even bear to watch certain films as I was affected by what was on screen. However, it also has a positive side. It is super easy to be motivated to complete tasks when the outcome of not doing it would cause pain and hurt.

So, there I was, controlling my addictions and not drinking. I was taking control of my spiritual development and learning new skills. I was eating healthier and exercising more, but I was also balancing my new control ticks and mental stability throughout it all. A tightrope circus act, I was not, but I was soon learning to walk a fine line. On the one hand, I was recovering from addiction and had a new medical issue that was forming, and on the other hand, I was growing spiritually and mastering the dark voices.

It was clear that my life was looking very different from what it once used to be; I had made positive changes and taken big strides in my development. All that was needed now was a new job. That is when I contacted Mercedes to inform her that I wanted to return to being a trainer. I sent off my CV and was offered an interview in November 2007, which I obviously crushed as they made me an offer within the hour. The new job was working as an employment coach within the private sector, supporting others to find sustainable jobs. This next step would be a serious job, no cocaine for breakfast was allowed at this place, and in this job, alcoholics didn't get promoted either; instead, alcoholics got sacked!

Chapter 9

Walking to my new job was petrifying. I had on a nice suit, and my power girl badass walk was off to a T. I was placed with a colleague called Andrew, and my assignment was to follow him around all day and learn the job. Well, that sounded easy enough. I was in a rundown building next to Fratton Bridge Centre, the paint had marks all down it, and graffiti was scribbled all over the walls. There was this smell wherever I walked - in the hallway, the multiple rooms and offices. If I closed my eyes and I took a deep inhale, it was like I was inside a 14-year-old's armpit after sports day. With a faint whiff of baked goods and farts all mixed together, it was like the perfect concoction to knock out a horse. My word, did it stink; it hummed like a motherfucker!

I must have been introduced to around ten or so staff, and in one room alone, they had around fifty plus people. Working over time, I would see many of the same characters, from the unshaven old man wearing a bright yellow workman coat, to the baseball cap-wearing youngster in a tracksuit. There were various groups or provisions for unemployed people, all on different programmes, depending on their claim status. A few rooms had computers and telephones, I assumed for job searching, and each desk had enough paperwork to sink a large ship.

My head was spinning as I witnessed the arguments and battles between the tutors and clients. One guy had a knife hidden in the skirting board in one of the rooms! They couldn't prove it was his, so he was allowed to stay on the course. This place was crazy, like a cattle herd of all the smelly and lazy people crammed into the same room.

I felt sorry for the odd few people there who really did want to get a job; clients were mandated by their benefit officers to attend the courses and to gain employment. If clients were kicked off the programmes, their benefit money was stopped, and many of the faces in each room were already making a career out of not working. It was all very new to me; I was being informed of documents and courses that I had never even heard of. All the paperwork and documents were legal requirements, leaving no room for error. I sat in the largest room, watching all the clients leave for their lunch break, and then witnessed their audacity as 99% of them strolled straight into the pub across the road. I laughed to myself because we had a strict no-drinking policy. The only wiggle room was for heroin addicts who were allowed to leave and collect their methadone throughout the day.

Andrew was a relaxed and funny guy; he was nothing like me. He joked around and had slopey shoulders with his paperwork. The clients seemed to like him, and he was definitely a drinker. I could tell.

After the last client had left for the day, Andrew pulled out an ashtray from his desk drawer, and we smoked a well-deserved cigarette. I was glad that no one had recognised me throughout the day, as my previous circles did involve thieves, drug addicts and drinkers. Now, these were my new clients at work. I just prayed no one I had previously sold drugs to would walk through the door.

I was pretty frazzled by the end of the day, so I called my mother to moan about my new challenge. I smiled coyly as my mum reminded me of my previous fears from when I started working at the cafe years ago. I had to memorise a whole menu for a cafe and dining area, with all the variations, ingredients, and possibilities. With over three hundred various food combinations, plus beverages, it seemed doubtful I would ever memorise it all. I felt the task was too much, including knowing the cost price for each item needed for operating the cashier area. Of course, my mother was right; I did learn everything I needed to know and then some, and within no time, I was promoted and considered one of their best staff members. With my new confidence and attitude, kindly given by my mother, I was determined to learn as much as I could about this new job and be the best.

After my normal routine of exercise and eating dust, I knuckled down to some serious research. I saved everything I read to memory, and I even practised with my brother Brand. Soon, Brand was throwing work quiz questions my way, and I was knocking them out of the park.

I enjoyed the next few weeks of shadowing in my new role. I picked up new information fast, and I caught on quick. I surprised most of the staff with my previous experience, especially my ability to speak in front of a class full of strangers while commanding the room. I had been a qualified trainer since I was seventeen years of age; I was no stranger to facing the dilemma of awkwardness that is produced when a person trains someone who is older. I also knew how to banter and speak the same dialect as the clients, which helped me. It is a fine art to dance between the waves of facilitator and friend, enforcer, and support network. I had to be a chameleon, switching between being an informer, educator, teacher, advisor and life coach. I was able to use keywords which would tell a person that I understood their situation all too well, without announcing to everyone that I had been a crazy, drug-taking, whiskey-drinking whore.

I had left school at a very young age, I was lucky that in the 90s, employers hired staff based on their banter, and I could talk my way into any job. On my CV, it read that I passed all my GCSEs with flying colours, no one ever asked to see them. I had volunteered at my mother's charity shops which gave me work experience and an employment history for my CV. I also used to sell mobile phone tariff cards to my school friends, the tariff was fake, but my God, I made some money. I would tell kids that I could make them fake identifications, and, while in my Business Studies class, I would replace a tiny digit on their birth certificate and photocopy it. I would continue to make copies of each copy until the outline of the added number disappeared, and there you go; Mr XXX was now legally able to buy fags and alcohol. I had always been conniving and streetwise, and money-making schemes came to me as easy as air did. They say you can't blag a blagger, and it's true because we can detect bullshit a mile away.

I was soon recognised for my talents, and most of my ticks and medical issues generally went unnoticed. I could pace up and down while teaching a class, tap my fingers and stare at the ceiling undetected. Between the clients' hate for being placed on the course and their daily drama and antics, my behaviour and ticks were small fry in comparison.

I found that my life was improving greatly, and the fact I now worked with my best friend Mercedes was definitely the icing on top of my red velvet cake. I didn't get along with everyone I worked with; I feel this is because HATERS ARE GONNA HATE. I find people either love me or despise me, generally through jealousy and sheer lack of their own self-esteem. I am okay with this, I have tried to tone it down over the years, but when I forcefully tried to make myself smaller, I always failed. However, with age and wisdom, I have now adjusted naturally. This has not been forced, but it is genuine growth as a human being.

I soon was introduced to Robert. He was an ex-navy, die-hard type of guy. He was missing his front teeth and liked a sherbet or two, if you catch my drift. He delivered a different programme to me, but did I have to listen to his drone through the thin walls? The paint probably peeled itself off the wall in an attempt at suicide just to flake out his drooling blah blah blah. He worked with two other tutors delivering his course: a small, round lady called Ann, who was the daughter of a vicar, and a super overweight guy called Roger. Between them, they were a trio you didn't want to mess with. Robert would bore you to tears while Ann tried to save your soul. Roger just watched from a distance giving off his depressive energy. I worked with Roger for many years, and not once did I ever see him walk anywhere or arrive. The chair would be empty, and then, like magic, he would be sat in it. Fast forward eight hours, and like a puff of smoke, he was gone.

I worked on another course within the same building, and it wasn't long before I was trained up and ready to sparkle. I designed my first training lesson for the course, which was based on hygiene - not for clients who were keen to work in the catering industry but for themselves. It wasn't fair to make everyone breathe in the same stinky air; you could taste each other's feet with each inhale, and it was not okay. Some of the clients on the programme were lovely people who washed their hair, brushed their teeth and wore clean clothes. Unfortunately, those clients were one in every hundred!

I seemed to have found my style at work, and no, I don't mean my outfit. I was strict in the classroom but fair. I enforced the rules, and I had empathy to give when needed. I was engaging too, but to be fair, the bar was set pretty low as far as other tutors were concerned. All I had to do was not be depressing, refrain from saving any souls and not bore them death and winner, winner chicken dinner. It must have helped that I am not exactly garbage to look at. I have been told that I am very animated, which is apparently very entertaining.

I settled in nicely at work, and at home, I was kickboxing with Sammy and the girls, which helped my anxiety. My anxiety fears would whisper in my ear, "They can see you shaking, and they know you are a mess." I would listen as I am not rude, but as time moved on, I would squash the voices, and no matter what happened, I refused to give up. Fake it until you make it is a popular saying, and I flew through the days with that motto clenched tightly in my fist. After throwing up my guts in the toilet, I would wipe my mouth and return to my classroom. As I shook like a tumble dryer, I still stood in front of the clients to teach. My motivation and determination to not give up were phenomenal. My daily shaking and vomiting increased and decreased throughout the week; it was part of the norm for me.

When I was an alcoholic, there were times, at the beginning, when I would lay my head down, and the room would spin. The saliva in my mouth would increase, and that voice in my head would say, "Oh fuck, I am gonna be sick." I would speak back to that voice, commanding it to stay in bed and sleep and swallow down any urges to be sick.

I cannot recall how long this went on until one day, no matter how much I drank, the need to vomit would never come to me. I could down a few litres of whiskey and not feel sick. I would drink and drink, and the only time sickness came a-knocking was when I needed another drink as it had been too long. It was that same voice inside my head that would tell me to keep going, not to give up or go home. I felt that I had to ride out the vomiting and shaking, and it may take me years, but no way was I giving up. For me, to go home was to give in to the illness. If I was to walk home and bail on my work, then the chances were it would happen again and again. Until one day when I would be Stay at Home Bryony, who doesn't leave her room. Well, not on my watch, pussy.

Not all days were horrific; some were okay, and, on the odd occasion, I would only vomit once or twice a day. My body shaking would depend on my mental state, environment and stress levels, so that fluctuated greatly too.

The day my supernatural gift infiltrated my day job was a shockingly strange day. It was a Monday morning, and the year was 2008. Andrew had called in sick, and it was new starter's day, so the office was buzzing with people and worried voices. Every week on Monday, new clients were mandated to attend our course. It was vital that each person signed some stupid document that we called 'Starter Paperwork.' I know, how imaginative, right?

With Andrew off work ill, I was called to step up and rise to the challenge. I was already feeling sick, and the thought of being solely responsible for all the legal paperwork was daunting. I was expecting over sixty clients, but they never all turned up. This Monday was particularly busy; I already had clients standing as all the chairs were occupied. I was sitting at my desk with a line of people outside the room; I only lifted my head to ask the next person's name. Once I rifled through hundreds of papers, I would ask them to sign and take an imaginary seat. Imagine you are a tutor on a course, with all eyes just staring at you, sending hateful vibes, with the attitude and body language to match.

The room was always a tough place to be, especially at the start of a course. The first few days were always with clients testing you and pushing, waiting for you to either break or kick them off the course. After a few days, the class settled down, and it got slightly easier: barriers were established, and standards set.

I remember lifting my head and gawking in absolute shock.

My mouth dropped open, and I said aloud, "But you are dead."

The room was silent as the man stood at the front of the queue. I blinked and blinked, but he was still standing there before me.

I turned towards the others, all sat in chairs and stood leaning against the walls, and asked, "Can you see him?"

A few heads just looked over me, a few said yes, and others just peered through me with daggers.

I turned my face back to Rick, thinking, 'I must be seeing a spirit as corporeal, bright as day. If I continue talking to him aloud, the clients will think I am mental. If I ignore him, but he is real, then a scene will unfold.' I was screwed no matter what decision I made. My brain was racing at a hundred miles an hour. Rick was dead, and he had been for a few years now. Confusion was hugging me like a pair of tights; what the hell was going on?

I spoke aloud again. "But you are dead. You died."

Rick looked at me, his mouth smiled, and he said, "I know."

Somehow, he then disappeared. I looked around at the faces of the clients, who didn't seem perplexed at all, and they still had the same look of disgust and anger on their faces. I didn't even have time to process what had happened, as I couldn't. In front of me was a class of fresh meat to break in and a million tasks to complete before the first break at 10.45 am.

I was not a stranger to seeing spirits, but I had been informed years ago about Rick hanging himself. It was a big deal, and I had worked with him in another job in a restaurant years ago.

I thought I had the voices and spiritualism under control, but clearly, I still had a lot to learn. I had conquered the dark voices, but now my supernatural encounters were encroaching in my place of work. I cannot imagine any person being at their happiest when unemployed and mandated to attend an employment course. Most of my clients were addicts, depressed, and definitely not in the best state of mind. Some were completely off their heads; we did have sex offenders sent to us, too, which was usually always disturbing. One guy used to draw pictures of the staff and hand them to us on scrap paper while talking about his mother in a sexual way. One client used to have sex in the toilet with everyone who winked at her, and another guy used to smell other people's hair. The building was full of people and their energy. I still wasn't perfect at protecting my own energy, and at times, I would pick up on others' vibes. I felt I needed help in this area, so my search began for a workshop on spiritualism.

Chapter 10

It was a Saturday, and I woke up feeling excited. Not only was it a non-workday, but I was enrolled on a special workshop on spiritualism. My niece Kayleigh had spotted the course a few days ago; it was announced after a demonstration of mediumship at the Portsmouth Temple of Spiritualism. The guy in question was amazing; he was proving with every message to people in the audience that life after death really did exist. One lady who was wearing a purple top was nodding in agreement as the man on the platform stage spoke of detailed places and people. There was no way he could have guessed any or all of the complicated evidence that he supplied.

His name was Paul Cissell, and he was young for a clairvoyant. Usually, the guest speakers were over a certain age; I assumed at the time that this was because age and time were needed - it takes time to learn such a complex skill and wisdom to tread the choppy waters of working for spirit. You do meet and hear of younger clairvoyants, so it is not unheard of, but it's not as common as a lady or gentleman over fifty years of age working on the platform. Paul had an energy about him; I felt drawn to him at the time and for a good reason too.

Kayleigh looked like a whale; she had a leopard print dress jumper on and obviously a push-up bra. She was heavily pregnant with her first baby; we were expecting a bouncing baby boy any day now. I say WE and not her because she relied on me to fill in for the baby's father. He was gone in the wind, like a leaf blowing down the road to freedom. Kayleigh was a demanding spoilt little cow bag who fleeced me more than the taxman did each month. If Kayleigh wanted a nice shiny pair of shoes, you could bet your bottom dollar that it would be me who would end up paying for them. I could never say no to her; it just wasn't in my vocabulary.

At only three years younger than me, our dynamic of Aunty and Niece was probably unusual to others. She played me like a violin, and I protected her fiercely, friends would refer to us as cousins, yet my sister Vikki is her mum. Our wisdom and knowledge were far from parallel to each other; I was the all-seeing eye, and she was a wandering blind chicken. Yet I would gut anyone like a fish if they even looked at her the wrong way. I definitely had no part to play in her latest predicament, yet here I was, buying her baby clothes, new carpets and nappies. The best way to describe her is to imagine a toddler that is loud and demanding, unafraid to throw a tantrum. Now all we have to do is swap the bottle of juice for a bottle of vodka and replace all the toys with men, clothes, shiny objects and perfume. Most people are afraid to upset Kayleigh as she is a strong personality, with big blue eyes and olive skin, courtesy of her Greek biological father. At least at the workshop, Kayleigh would have to shut her mouth for most of the day, leaving less opportunity for her classic comments to get us into hot water.

I didn't really know what to expect when I first walked into Paul's house in Portsmouth; it was a typical looking building. There were no bones hanging from the doorway, no black cat with an eye missing patrolling the halls, nor a garden cemetery. Instead, we walked into a lounge with many mix-and-match chairs placed strategically around the edge of the room. There was a mixture of both men and women, ranging from my niece's age of twenty-four all the way up to retirement age. One lady was wearing a deep velvet purple wrap-around scarf; she had kind eyes and short, dyed red hair. I was ecstatic.

I could tell Paul was going to teach me something new and leave me with a deeper understanding of my gift. To warm up, we did the usual introductions and shared our hopes for the day, followed by a few breathing techniques and a simple guided meditation. I spotted a plant in the corner of the room and many other natural items dotted around the house. Little did I know that we would be holding the items and reading their energy to see if we could share knowledge about them. It was amazing to be in a room with like-minded people; no one looked like a witch from a horror film, as some people may assume. Witchcraft is whole other practice. Yes, there are common crossovers between all religions and beliefs, but witchcraft is not spiritualism.

I needed all my energy currently being used to contain my gift, to evaporate and allow me to dive into the supernatural like a dolphin dipping for pearls. My skin was humming with the high energy in Paul's house. He was kind and relatable, and when he spoke, you could tell he knew something you didn't - like he had all the gossip or knew an inside joke. There was nothing unusual about Paul; he wasn't wearing a t-shirt that read, 'I have conversations with dead people.' Paul wore blue jeans and a knitted jumper. His smile was inviting, and his laugh was infectious. He is a really nice, genuine guy.

There was no competition in the room, but I noticed that many others only offered short answers to the tasks. I decided to keep my answers to a minimum, too; I didn't want to take over the group as I knew my personality could be strong. As the day progressed, I never wanted it to end. Paul started to smile wide as he was explaining the next task, and he struggled to contain his laughter. Later I would learn that Paul is a bit of a joker and no stranger to tricking his students in jest.

I stupidly volunteered to be the guinea pig, and I was swiftly asked to leave the room. I heard whispers and movement coming from the lounge, but there was no point in taking a peak, as it may have ruined the task. After being ushered back into the room, I noticed an empty chair at the front of the circle of faces, clearly left vacant for me. Instructions were given for me to sit in the seat and to feel the energy; everyone was looking at me expectantly to share any knowledge I may receive. As I sat down, I felt fat, like super oversized, so my eyes scanned the room, searching for any overweight possibilities. I didn't want to come across as rude, so I opted to say that I felt uncomfortably large; the tasks were hard. There were many things that I could have done or said, but I gave up and retained my old seat. Paul revealed that the person who had sat in the chair before me was Kayleigh, my pregnant niece. She laughed and leaned towards me afterwards; she seemed to be enjoying the day too. It was fascinating to watch others perform the same task after me; it really did push me to question where I was getting my instant knowledge or information from?

Towards the end of the day, we were set into small groups, and we were asked to read an object belonging to the other person. Known as a Psychometry reading, this skill was a task I had tried to do before. I held tightly onto a gentleman's ring, and I could smell the earth. I announced that he was a gardener and specifically that he had an allotment. Tomatoes popped into my head, and I felt sadness about a dilemma relating to his son. I was pleased when he confirmed all of this was right; he filled in the gaps and explained to me how it all made sense to him. Wahoo, I was on fire, metaphorically speaking.

As we sat in our small groups in the lounge, Paul tapped me on the shoulder and said, "I like your energy; I would like to invite you to join my development group."

My heart skipped a beat as I realised that Paul must have been impressed by me, or he at least felt I had a skill worth developing. There was no time for me to give an answer as Paul quickly turned back to address the group again. It all made sense to me now; I was supposed to meet Paul as he was an experienced teacher who trained and developed others. In my opinion, Paul was good, but I didn't quite realise just how good and world-renowned he was.

As Kayleigh and I walked outside, the fresh air hit me like a slap in the face while we scratched around for our cigarettes in our purses. Like a schoolgirl in love, I shared my invite with Kayleigh, and she was just as thrilled as I was for me. In the cold air of the night, both of us stood shivering in the dark on the streets of Portsmouth. As we eagerly waited for our taxi to take us home, once again, I felt hopeful.

My pillow felt cold and soft; my head and body were tired from the workshop. I closed my eyes and fantasised about my new path I was about to walk with Paul; the possibilities were endless.

I was still attending church on a Wednesday evening, but I mostly paid attention to the guests on the platform. I wanted to test my abilities, so I would open up my chakras, ground myself, and lift my vibration before taking the short walk to church. As I walked into the church, I would feel my skin hum; I loved the energy within the downstairs church hall. As I sat eagerly waiting in my seat, I wasn't ever hoping for a message from spirit like the other attendees. I was there to learn and practice.

I would tune into my gift to see if I could tell which person from the audience the medium would point at next? My predictions were nearly always spot on. I would also gaze around the room with a distant look, seeking any messages or clues from the environment. One thing I do recall is the dots. I always assumed that the reason I saw little dots in the room was due to my drug antics. Back in the day, when I was on drugs, especially while taking speed, I once held out my hand in an attempt to grab hold of wall-to-wall cling film that was all the way across the room. It looked like cling film because I was seeing dots, and the dots were vibrating so fast that an illusion of thin plastic was in my sight. After taking a street value of a few hundred pounds worth of speed, I accepted this cling film to be a hallucination caused by swallowing too many drugs.

I still see dots to this day, but while I was attending church, the dots increased dramatically. It didn't take long for me to piece it together; when I was working supernaturally, I could also see these dots. Once I made this connection between the dots and the spirit world, I began analysing the dots' behaviour; this opened my eyes to a whole new area. Whenever I walked into a room, I could sense what the dots' actions were telling me. Sometimes they were faster in movement, and at other times, the number of dots would differ too. The higher the energy level was, the faster the dots would move. I noticed there were more dots when the energy increased, but it could have just appeared that way due to the dots vibrating faster.

I could be in another person's house and just watch the energy dots fly around the rooms. It did become distracting at times, but it was fascinating too. If I became overwhelmed by the dots, at times, I questioned the reality of my surroundings. I honestly occasionally believed that I could put my hand through a solid piece of furniture, as what I was seeing were the dots of energy around it. Nothing ever looked solid. One example is to compare my experience to the Keanu Reeves film, The Matrix, when Neo starts seeing the code instead of his usual vision. That is probably a bad example, but you get the idea. Even though my brain knew the furniture was real and solid, another part of my brain questioned this as my vision was altered. The perfect example that only people over a certain age will be able to comprehend is to picture the static on the television. Static on the big box was hundreds of little dots moving and flashing; my dots were similar but more transparent. The dots would come and go, but the more I developed my supernatural gift, the longer their appearances would last.

None of the visual changes helped with my state of mind when I was having a bad day. It is easy to question your own sanity when watching dots chase around. My friends and family probably hardly noticed my hand slowly reaching out to grab various items. I was caught a few times at work banging my fingers into walls while staring intently at the paint and plaster. No one ever questioned me, though; I guess most people are drowning in their own thoughts and problems.

It was in my new job role that I met a colleague; she was from Spain and had wild curly brown hair. She wore long skirts and purple tops, with beaded bracelets and a crystal necklace. One may have called her a hippie, but she was a spiritualist. We would talk between classes, and it was this beautiful lady who helped me to make a realisation. When I would speak of my past antics of alcohol and drugs, I would refer to myself as 'old Bryony.' It was like I felt I was a new person, and it was an attempt to detach myself from my previous behaviours and indiscretions. My new friend explained that this would cause a conflict within me and that acceptance of my past would offer both peace and strength. In a stupid way, I thought that because I had changed, I was no longer that drunken whore bitch. But for me to wipe all of my past history away was to deny myself the triumph and glory of my growth. I understand the importance of this simple act, to own my mistakes and troubles. Now, I am proud to tell others about my past and wear the stereotype as a badge of honour and scars from my inner battled war.

I struggled against prejudiced doctors, and I still do to this day. A few years ago, I attended the doctor's surgery with the symptoms of severe headaches and blurred vision. And the only response I received was an appointment for bloods to check on my liver count. I am not embarrassed or ashamed of my life and journey, but the stigma around addiction and mental health is still very real to this day. Obviously, I do not disclose my life story at job interviews, but I do share it with everyone else in the world. If my story and experiences can help others, then who am I to hold this information hostage?

As the next few weeks went by, I looked forward to my Thursday evenings with Paul's group. I loved learning more each week and developing my skills. I still enjoyed my kickboxing classes, and my mind was becoming stronger each day. However, it felt like the stronger my body and mind became, the more new medical conditions would arise. It is not easy recovering from addiction, especially when every doctor I met seemed to have the same attitude. The most common response was that issues and tissues were normal after giving up alcohol and drugs. I can see their point of view; I was just a shaking time bomb who inflicted all my issues on myself.

At least it was Thursday; my development started at seven o'clock, and my God, I needed it. Spiritualism helps me to focus and to see the bigger picture. I needed spiritualism. I was committing to this new path, no matter and wherever it may lead me.

As I walked into work, my hands were vibrating; at the time, I didn't originally understand why. All I had to do was get through the next eight hours, and then this evening, I would attend Paul's group. A pattern was starting to form that every week on the same day, my hands vibrated; it was bewildering. I would wake up feeling excited, and my stomach felt like it had butterflies inside. As the day dragged on, my energy levels felt higher instead of lower throughout the shift. This feeling continued every Thursday for many years later. I can only assume that this was due to my continuous attendance at the development group, working with spirit throughout each evening.

Nothing exciting happened on this particular shift; I mean, we did have the usual fights and clients being kicked off the course. We had to hire a security guard in the end as the violence increased; it always made me laugh when someone got up in my face. I used to smile because outside of work, I would smash their face in if they attacked me. I might be a spiritualist, but I am no pushover; I do not condone fighting, but I do believe in defending oneself. I can count on one hand the total number of times I have thrown a pre-emptive strike; any other fight I have had has always been in self-defence. It always rattled my cage because these idiots would be aggressive, squaring up to me or Mercedes, yet outside the classroom, they wouldn't dare.

I did have this one guy that was locked outside of a room because he was being threatening; unfortunately, he was locked in the stairwell with me. He spat towards my face and repeatedly kicked the door while shouting that he was going to kill me! A team member telephoned the police, and I stood my ground, praying that this lairy git would throw a punch. We were allowed to defend ourselves against an attack at work; he didn't physically touch me, to my disappointment. He soon got tired and walked down the stairs to the exit, and the police finally arrived, albeit the next day! I was always shocked by the behaviour of some of these men; I did see the git again outside of my work while I was with Brand. My brother Brand goes to the gym every day and is over 6 feet tall; when the git spotted me, he began to swagger in my direction. But as soon as he spotted my brother, he turned and walked the other way.

I used to moan to Mercedes all the time, sharing the fact that I had never even heard any of my brothers raise their voices to a female. Yet each day in class, we were threatened and verbally abused; one crackhead girl even attacked me in a nightclub! I was on the lemonade and able to walk into clubs without being too tempted by the drink; in fact, it helped me at times. I would watch others getting smashed, and as I witnessed the cattle market of drunks dancing, I would feel pride in my sobriety. I was in Chicago Rock when the crackhead shouted at me. I had recently kicked her off the employment course, and she blamed me. She was like a dwarf at four foot nothing, and there I was, a kickboxer at five foot seven. She ran towards me, and I just held my hand at arm's length; she couldn't reach me. I didn't even want to hit her for her attack; it didn't seem fair with the size difference.

I had more serious attacks at work and a few close calls too. This one guy hated me immensely; I didn't even know him or teach him in my class. Yet he kept bad-mouthing me, and he used to walk into our offices and scream at the top of his voice, "I am gonna kill Bryony." One day he kept telling others who were outside smoking that he was going to kill me; luckily, they informed me, and the police were called. It was scary to be informed that the police arrested him outside of my work; he had various weapons and a razor blade on him. I suppose all this drama may sound exciting, but you get used to it in the end.

My employer enrolled me on a teaching course with Kingston University, which I passed easily. I have always been a trainer, but it was definitely informative to learn about the educational side of things. I later signed up for a two-year course at Surrey University to become a qualified teacher. During the riots in London, I also attended and completed a Security Officer course; my employer figured that if they trained a staff member, they wouldn't need to pay a separate security officer. I was never easily intimidated by the antics or threats from these men; years of working in pubs and clubs had given me experience in dealing with conflict management. It helped that I had always managed to be involved with fighting - as a child all the way up to adulthood.

This next fact will either shock or amaze you; I have had more fights with men than with women! I was put in hospital at age fourteen after losing my first ever fight. I have had my head smashed open with bottles, and I have had my head kicked in by various groups. I must sound like a nutcase, but the truth was that people just wanted to fight me a lot as a child. My father was a strict man, and he warned me that if I ever came home with a black eye, the other kid had better look worse.

I was taught to defend myself; it was the eighties, and I was raised to hit back. The secret is that when you are fighting, you can't feel any pain, not really. The adrenaline coursing through your body sees to that, and once you are no longer scared of getting hit, the conflict seems less scary. I also was raised with two of my three older brothers in the house; Brand is now big and strong, similar to Arren. I looked like Arren when I was younger, but now, I am just as tall as him, if not taller! They terrorised me as a kid, locking me outside the house all day, naked. They once tied me up with rope in the garden and left me there all day.

However, the scariest has to be between the tumble dryer and the freezer. They tricked me into proving that I could fit into the tumble dryer, and once I was inside, they slammed the door closed. The dryer started spinning round and round. The inside had these spike bits that stuck out; I would spin to the top and then drop. I remember looking outside the hole in the wall where the condensation pipe exited. I kept thinking, 'At least I won't die, as oxygen can still get in.' Luckily, Arren shit his pants and told my mum, who came to free me from the ordeal.

Another time, Brand dared me to bite the freezer, so I did. It was petrifying as my lips were frozen to the edge of the shelf. Brand went all tense, and I could tell he was scared. As I pulled away from the freezer, my mouth was stuck, attached by the inside section of my lips. Brand ran off to fetch a glass of water, but in my scared state, I ripped my lips off! My lips poured with blood from the inside, and my mouth tissue was stuck on the edge of the freezer shelf.

So, you see, I have been training for others to terrorise me my whole life, and you know how the saying goes? Whatever doesn't kill you makes you stronger. Growing up with three older brothers was horrible at the time, but now I have three protectors who help me out when needed. The combination of brothers terrorising me and all the fights I endured from childhood made me a strong person. I guess getting beaten with a leather belt helped me, too, as there isn't much in life that scares me, if I am honest. I assume all my experiences in life are what made me good at this new job, and it didn't hurt that I left school early, either.

When a client would argue the point with a tutor, they were used to winning their battles by playing the druggy card. No card won arguments with me, for I was an ex-druggy, an ex-alcoholic and an early school leaver who had multiple medical conditions. I was a good teacher who took a holistic approach, I did want to help people learn the correct skills to find themselves a job, but I also wanted to address the underlining cause of their long-term unemployment. I started teaching classes on developing motivation and confidence, and I soon became a qualified goals trainer, a course designed around letting go of baggage. This included clients and students setting themselves realistic goals and making life-changing habits. It was this new approach combined with the routine classes which really had a dramatic effect on a person's attitude and life.

I hear the church clock chime; it must be home time.

Nearly time for my next class with Paul ...

Chapter 11

Six months later ....

The past six months have been a rollercoaster of a ride; I have been rocking it at Paul's development group.

My new job is also going fantastic; I am born again like a caterpillar that has transformed into a butterfly, floating on the currents. I have been feeling confident in my new skin, with a new awareness of other entities and the supernatural. I was ecstatic.

Pounds of fat have dropped off of me faster than a lorry tumbles off a cliff – dramatically. My weekends consist of going to parties and nightclubs; I can walk into a bar and order a glass of lemonade like a boss. My kickboxing schedule is strategically planned for the weekends, too, to add another bonus and deterrent from any lures of the whiskey and booze.

Do not be mistaken; the drink still sings to me like a siren in the big ocean, promising me sweet nothings with her mesmerising song. She calls to me, singing her lullaby and pulling me towards her dark depths of the void, but I turn away and fight the urges she births inside me. It is strange that I do not find myself missing the drugs. I long for the escape, but I am focusing my energy on building a life that dispels my need to find a new dimension. I have never believed that running away is ever the way forward. 'Water the grass where you live' has always been my motto.

I cannot decide what to wear tonight. With plans to sleep at Kayleigh's house, I am definitely in for a night of antics. What age do we ever really grow up? My time with Kayleigh is always filled with childish jokes and light-hearted fun. It will be interesting to see what her new house is like.

When I arrived at the new house in Portsmouth, it was rather nice; large and empty, but it will do for her, and it was close to the train station and shops. The evening was comforting, with a feeling of ease and safety, which I only have with a handful of humans. As I laid my head down on the chilly pillow in Kayleigh's bed, my mind started to drift towards tomorrow's lesson plans for work.

A clock was ticking loudly, which was distracting me from my thoughts when I heard a toy from downstairs being played with. Lee-Connor was fast asleep in his bedroom, directly opposite the room we were in. Ignoring the noise was no use as the toys banging and crashing became unbearable.

I nudged Kayleigh to alert her. "Kayleigh, can you hear the toys being played with downstairs?"

The silence was not reassuring. She replied, "What are you on about, you din?"

"The toys downstairs, someone is playing with them; I can hear the music and shit. Go and move them."

Her voice rose high like a squeaky mouse. She had no intention of walking downstairs to stop the noise that she couldn't hear. As she hugged the cover toward her face, she hid her eyes with the bedsheets. It was driving me nuts. I knew it was a supernatural happening, and all I wanted was some damn sleep!

"There is a baby crying now, Kayleigh. Just go downstairs and move them fucking toys. Come on!"

Kayleigh sounded stubborn and petrified. She argued with me, saying that she didn't want to investigate the sound, and a few leg strikes were exchanged between us.

I begged her to move them. From my point of view, she had nothing to fear as she couldn't hear anything anyway! On the other hand, I was bombarded with the creepy chime of toys bashing together, and undoubtedly if I walked down the stairs, I would be faced with a vision that I really did not want to see. I could already feel my other senses increase their activation levels. I knew the baby had died and a fire had been involved; flashes of someone else's memories were infiltrating my mind's eye. Closing my eyes was about as much use as a chocolate teapot, but I tried it anyway. It was useless fighting against it, so I began to share the knowledge I had with Kayleigh, which just made things worse, and I ended any hopes I had of her tiptoeing down the staircase.

An hour can feel like an eternity when you are trying to sleep, an endless pit of baby cries echoing from the darkness and penetrating my space like an invader. Eventually, I must have fallen asleep, but I never slept at that particular house again.

A pattern was occurring within my day-to-day life. The more I learnt and the deeper I walked down the rabbit hole, the more strongly my connection to the spirit world was becoming. Paul had a different view on switching off to the spirit world; he believed we could never really turn it off. My first development circle spoke about climbing inside a box or bin and that closing the lid would stop any supernatural connection. It was Paul who said we could turn the volume down on the spiritual senses, and when wanting to tune in, we could turn the dial up. This was an area I seemed to be struggling with. I appeared to always be on high alert, and at times, I couldn't differentiate between the living people and the dead!

My employer decided that I would be perfect for working on a new outreach programme, travelling between local areas to deliver employment courses in various buildings. I was assigned to Havant, Fareham, Gosport and Cosham. In Fareham, I worked inside this large building above the high street shops; it was a church organisation of some kind. After walking through a large hall, I was faced with two small rooms; the corner room looked like a nursery with toys and a chalkboard.

In Gosport, my courses were delivered inside a small centre where we hired a room from some group. It was a tiny unattractive space; it was depressive with bright luminescent lights. I didn't much care for catching a ferry over from Portsmouth; as a non-driver, it was a mission while carrying hundreds of documents.

I was never booked to attend the Cosham building, but I will never forget the Havant one ...

As I disembarked the train in Havant, it was raining heavily. Thank God it was, as I was hoping to get soaking fucking wet for the day. I dashed through the streets in the town centre as fast as I could while carrying fifteen plus files. As I arrived at the church, it was modern looking, with glass windows instead of the usual flint blocks. Internally, it looked like a café, but a posh one, with a few tables and chairs inside the door. It was carpeted in a blue, fuzzy fabric like you would find in any English school. A spiral staircase curved and twisted, allowing access to the first floor, and a large, open-plan space was looking back at me.

My hands started to vibrate like they do every Thursday. Oh no, I could feel my spiritual side starting to activate. With fifteen clients due to start their employment course in less than thirty minutes, I concentrated on preparing the room. It was like a challenge I was not supposed to succeed with. I had no printer or computer, no telephone line in sight and no resources at all; this course was doomed. Shit, shit, fucking shit. I have been royally stitched up with this one. If only I could find the unhelpful woman who greeted me downstairs, then maybe I could borrow some equipment? After wandering through the grey looking rooms, I found a platform; I assume it was used for services as it was like a stage with seating surrounding it. Finally, I located the receptionist in a small room staring at a wall; she looked like she was in a daze.

"Hello, sorry to disturb you again, but do you have a telephone or printer in this building? And a computer would be great."

I don't think she liked me being there, as she turned and gave me this stare like I was a meatball in her vegetable pasta. Slowly her head began to shake from left to right absentmindedly; this was just another fantastic thing to happen today. Minus any equipment or resources, I was expected to deliver a course and help the unemployed apply for jobs. Perfect, just perfect!

The clock struck nine. I could hear the hustle of coats grazing against the wall and heavy footsteps on the stairs. It was not an easy pill to swallow as I explained that we would complete all theory-based sessions while I worked out the little problem of us having no equipment. Never mind the fact that it was compulsory for jobs to be applied for; they certainly wouldn't complete an online application here in this church. I decided to deliver a session on the open market; at least I could educate them on opportunities and avenues they may not have previously considered. My class was a mixture of sex offenders and long term unemployed. It was always sketchy when supporting any new group. A fight could explode at any moment, with a volatile atmosphere that usually settled over time.

As I stood in front of the class, pacing back and forth, I could see the reception lady in the corner of my eye. Stood to my right side, she waited quietly as I finished my sentence before turning my attention to her. With a flick of my hair, I raised my eyebrows to encourage her to speak, and in a flash, she disappeared. Within the blink of an eye, she just vanished; we were in a large room with one staircase in and out. There is no way she was secretly The Flash - or was she?

I quickly returned to my class, and all was forgotten; she was a strange lady indeed. As my day ended and the rain had finally let up, I was free. Carrying my files and bag, I descended the staircase, and I spotted a gentleman in his late forties or early fifties behind the sign-in desk. He looked a bit more with it than the other lady had; maybe he could locate some office equipment?

"Excuse me, sir. Do you happen to have any printers, computers or telephones in this building that I could borrow tomorrow?"

He looked baffled for a moment or two before responding. "None that are working. The internet has been playing up for a while now, but you could use the printer in the administrator's room."

Thank the Lord; at least I would be able to make copies of my documents.

"That would be great; thank you so much. I will see you tomorrow morning. Can you let the other lady who works here know as well, please?"

"What other lady? I am the only person who works here on a Monday."

As the penny dropped, I must have looked dumb-faced as he just smiled and waved me goodbye. That lady was a spirit, yet she had looked as real to me as the building itself. When she moved, I had heard footsteps, hadn't I? Her voice was quiet but audible, and I had a feeling I would see her again real soon.

My place of employment wasn't free of imposing spirits anymore, just like my niece Kayleigh's house wasn't either. It was not that I didn't want to speak with any spirits, but when they just showed up at my place of work, it really was terrible timing. However, I did welcome one particular lady who I first met at my sister Vikki's house in Milton Road in Portsmouth.

Vikki previously lived in Buckland for many years; in the nineties, the area had a bad reputation for crime and drugs. I suppose you get bad areas wherever you go, just like you hear about the nice ones too. Vikki moved away from Buckland in Portsmouth to Copnor; she was over the moon when she signed the paperwork for her new house. The day she unpacked her boxes, she was full of hope and anticipation; however, I was nowhere to be seen. It was a few days later when I walked through her front door to inspect the new digs and give it the once over.

Milton Road was a busy one-way street, and at the time, it was home to Kingston Prison. It was a tall grey-looking building that, back then, had housed many B/C category prisoners since 2003. When it opened in 1877, it was for category A prisoners and looked like a church at the entrance. Portsmouth has many areas, including Southsea seafront; it's beautiful there with a wonderful view of the Isle of Wight stretching from Eastney to Old Portsmouth. Southsea has a hovercraft that sails to swish you away across the choppy sea to the Isle of Wight, leaving the stone beach of Portsmouth for the golden sands at Ryde harbour. We have a great fairground at Southsea with lots of rides and arcade machines, like any other seaside town, I guess.

In the winter, the beach looks pretty in its own way but come summertime, the beach and multiple grass areas are full of families and friends. The alluring smell of BBQ food cooking is always lingering, mixed with the heat and sea air, which is intoxicating. At Castle Fields, we attend festivals and concerts next to a leisure centre in the shape of a blue glass pyramid. The pyramids or glasshouse, as it is also known to be called, is surrounded by the most stunning rock garden, with ponds and wildlife around every nook and cranny. It is a short stroll to the skate park and tennis courts, with play areas and a canoe lake. Southsea offers a variety of fun activities for all the family.

My sister's new house was on the opposite side of the street to the prison but a few doors down. She was smack bang in line with a pub called The Rose in June; she will undoubtedly be frequenting their establishment a few nights a week. I had drunk in that pub many times before; it had been owned since 2003 by a lovely couple called Caz and Paul. As I took my first step into the house, it was lovely, with laminate flooring and a large front room. The kitchen was small, but it bolted onto a dining room and a conservatory which allowed the sunshine to flood through. With a nice size garden, half concrete and half turf, it was perfect for BBQs and had enough grass for the two young boys to play football.

"I like it, Vikki," I told her. "I love the conservatory and garden, much better than the first floor flat at Buckland."

My sister nodded her head in agreement and invited me to view the bedrooms upstairs.

As we climbed the first few steps, that's when I first met her; she was small and frail like a bird. She appeared in a flash, and in an instant, she was gone. Unphased, I continued up the stairs while telling Vikki about her elderly guest. My sister didn't mind as she had always been interested in spiritualism. Vikki often took me to church over the past few years; she was also good friends in the past with psychic Dave too. With three spacious rooms and a large bathroom, they were onto a winner; it was definitely an upgrade.

Over the next few months, I became friends with the dead lady. She would share information with me, and I would eagerly pass it on to Vikki. I usually would see her when I was sitting on the sofa by the door, and she would make her presence known in other ways too. Unaccountable noises would happen when I was in the house, and if she didn't like something, I was able to tell. I often said to Vikki, "Did you do XXX the other day or move XXX?" I could be sitting on the sofa or a dining room chair, and the temperature would just drop around me. As a breeze chilled my arm, I would know she was there, wanting to talk. The lady wasn't evil, and she didn't harbour any malice toward us; she was just calling out for my attention. Who would want to be ignored all day? I bet she looked forward to my visits.

The real funny part is how common it was for me to talk to spirit while in the company of the living. I recall talking to the spirit lady while sitting on the stairs. My nephew Tray walked by me, and he must have been seven years old as the year was 2007/8, and he didn't even bat an eyelid. At the time I was talking aloud, he could hear a one-way conversation, and it was normal to him. "Aunty Bryony was talking to the dead," is what he would say; he never doubted it or questioned it. I did often wonder about my siblings with children; I was an addict and alcoholic who had visions and often talked aloud to the dead. Yet I was a brilliant Aunty who was often left in charge of the little munchkins, and if they left me with two kids, then two kids were returned. I never lost one or injured one; we always had fun and played games or decorated Dalek cakes. They didn't know 100% that I wasn't crazy, but they must have trusted my judgment and love for them all.

My brother Elijah has four children, Dayna, Den, Skye, and Mika. Arren has two sprogs nowadays with his beautiful wife Carrie, Bianca and Liam, not that I have ever looked after them. My two sisters who live in Essex have children, too; the eldest one is thirty-six years old,

I believe, and the youngest is eight. Mind you, I last saw them back in the year 2000, the millennium when we all feared our bank details would go bingo bango!

Now that I analyse it, Vikki is the only one who ever let me babysit her kids back then. I cannot compare the past with now, as I am a lot less crazy and high and much more responsible and sober. My niece Danni has allowed me to have her kids for days out and sleepover nights, and so has Kayleigh too.

My niece Dayna has just had a gorgeous baby girl with jet black hair; she looks just like her mum. The baby has big blue eyes that sparkle; with both parents having brown eyes, we were surprised, to say the least. Danni has two little ones called Kit and Sam; they both have beautiful hair and blue eyes. Kit has these curly locks that fall around her face, and Sam is a clever bunny who can read books way above his age group.

Lee-Connor and Esme are both beautiful, and when I say my great-nieces and great-nephews are beautiful, they truly are! Lee-Connor loves playing football and gaming; he is at that age, I guess, whereas Esme enjoys animal trails and the great outdoors. Esme has dark olive skin and warm coloured eyes; she is a chatterbox who loves to dance.

Dayna works as an airline hostess and has travelled the world, while her brother Den was into boxing, big time. Den has jet black hair and brown eyes like Dayna, I haven't seen him for years, but I hear he has a baby now. Arren's kids are such a work of art, they have a blond-haired and blue-eyed father, yet their mother is half Chinese with brown eyes, jet black hair and olive skin. Liam is olive-skinned with blue eyes, but Bianca has skin that is white as snow with blue eyes and light blonde hair. The combination of their mother and father's DNA is phenomenal; Carrie, their mum, is a clever lady with a taste for the finer things in life.

I am a very lucky person to be blessed with such wonderful children and now adults too in my family, Vikki's boy, Tray, is an adult now, and her youngest boy, Tru, will be seventeen soon. Her two eldest are Danni and Kayleigh, at thirty-two and thirty-five years of age: fully grown women now with their own children to nurture.

A few months later, I was itching to learn more and better myself, not just for my spiritual development but also to progress my career. So, this girl from Pompey decided to go to college. I was signed up and enrolled to attend college on a Wednesday evening; I was studying to be a qualified teacher. It was at college that I met Hannah, a short blonde bombshell. My God, she is a beautiful human being, both inside and out; she is the kind of person who will do anything for you. She is a drama teacher and has the biggest smile in the whole world. We instantly bonded, and her personality was just as crazy as mine; we found that we had loads in common. I liked to exercise and keep a critical eye on my weight, as did she. We both liked to laugh and go out and party. Hannah just got my sense of humour. Nine times out of ten, if I sniff another person's hair, they tend to roll their eyes and say, "WHAT THE FUCK ARE YOU DOING?" If I sniffed Hannah's hair, she'd respond with, "Oh babe, I've missed you." I can be honest to God weird when I want to be. I confuse others with my ability to turn into any character and respond with elaborate stories that couldn't be further from the truth, yet each story ends with me being asked by XXX, "When did that happen?"

For me, I can tell stories for hours. My sarcastic responses turn into sentences, paragraphs, and then full-page stories. Most of the time, my sense of humour flies over their head, and I spent the next six months keeping up a facade. After too much time has passed, it becomes too awkward to reveal the truth. I am not saying I am a liar, as I am honest to a fault. But if some douche decides to take my intended funny response about being vegetarian after witnessing me eat meat for several months seriously, then who am I to correct them?

Week after week, Hannah and I would sit and draw each other pictures or gossip - as girls do. We were once asked to draw a picture of ourselves. Our pictures were of fat girls with hairy legs. It is funny how we are engrained to notice our faults rather than celebrate our likes. I remember looking at a lady called Beth, who used to sit opposite me, and I noticed she had this energy about her. She never really spoke to me, and we were never friendly, but I could feel her pain crashing into me wave upon wave. I tried my hardest not to concentrate on her, but each time her emotions jolted me like an electric shock. I felt drawn to her with a need to ease her pain, but what would I say? I can hear it in my head now, "Hi, my name is Bryony, and I talk to the dead. I can feel your pain. Are you okay?" It sounded crazy, so of course, I wasn't going to approach her, but I did smile at her lots and send good vibrations her way.

This was just another example of how my development journey was intruding on my life. I definitely needed Paul to help me control this better. I had been in his class for a long time now, and I had made a deal with my spiritual guides that I was ready to go all the way on this path. When I meditated or was sitting alone at home, I would chat to them. My connection had strengthened so much that the speed of responses was so fast. In my head, I would ask my guides a question, but before I had even finished saying the request, I would receive the answer as instant knowledge. The speed was so quick that it was aggravating. At times, I felt stupid even starting the sentence. This is what led me to conclude that when I am speaking with my guides, they receive my questions at the thought process stage: the gap between a thought forming in my mind and the time when I ask the question in hand.

Some things never change, and I find this a comfort. Each night as I lay in bed, my mattress still bounces up and down. Get your mind out of the gutter, as I am referring to spirit children. I have experienced this since I was a little girl.

Life goes on, and time moves by like the seasons. Leaves fall off the trees, and in spring, the daffodils rise and fall. The next few years went by pretty fast for me; I decided to pour all my energy into working hard and learning more. My career rocketed in my new role as my success just went from good to excellent. I was the best in the business, and everyone knew it. My personal life was filled with exercising and training the girls for kickboxing, studying and composing lesson plans for college. I would wake up at 5 am and go for a run followed by a morning swim; I would then go to work and bosh it like a boss. After work, I would play football, go running and kickbox. I would attend Paul's development group on a Thursday, and I was thriving. I found it all so easy; I am good at most things. I had never failed a test, and I had not failed to receive a job offer after I applied for a new role. I was in a really good place mentally and physically. I finished paying off any money I owed to the bank, and life was great. My days were filled with goals and aims to meet and exceed, which I smashed daily.

I was still slightly damaged; I was frequently sleeping with multiple men, having sex with one guy in the morning and another in the afternoon. I couldn't bring myself to commit or open myself up to any type of hurt. The result was that I was a whore by name and a whore by nature, but my God, it was fun! Technically, I informed each of my men about one another, but for some reason, they just laughed like I was making a joke.

Between 2009 and 2012, I must have slept with over a hundred men, some were one-night stands, but a few were consistent. I was living my best life, having sex with a sexy drummer one night and a construction guy another. I am not judgemental at all; in fact, I would like to say that I am inclusive when it comes to sex, as, at the time, I would literally fuck anyone. Big guys, little guys, redheads, brunettes, long hair, no hair, curly hair, rough beards, skinny ones and big belly or webbed feet. I offered no promises, and in return, I was having the time of my life. Yet I still had wounds deep inside echoing through me like a never-ending bell. I was unstoppable and insatiable. I had this need for human contact but no ability to take it further with any man.

I signed up for more courses; I even passed my TEFL course after fantasising about myself in Italy as an English teacher. My friends surrounded me like primroses, close by and supportive. I enjoyed the stability of living at the house that I had moved to from my sister's place; I stayed there for a few years until 2011. My mates all rallied to help me when I made my next move to Granada Road in Southsea. My brother Brand broke up with his partner, so we found a flat to live in together. The flat was right next to the beach, it had super high ceilings, and it was perfect for us. It was exciting to go shopping for new furniture and decorate our flat to look super awesome. Brand has a very creative mind; we purchased essentials like a jukebox and an arcade machine with over eighty games on it. The walls were covered in canvasses of rock bands and coloured spotlights, and the kitchen had a keyboard across the breakfast bar. My brother's guitars were displayed artistically in the lounge, and we had front row seats to any drama and fights that might kick off in the street below. Clubbers often leave the pubs and bars nearby, and like clockwork, scraps and fights happened all along the street that we lived on. I could still walk to my day job, and the beach was less than 500 metres away.

My life was looking good and feeling great; it absolutely rocked to be me. I also felt comfortable with my spiritual knowledge and abilities, but little did I know that a new challenge was waiting just around the corner.

Chapter 12

As the sun leaked in through my window, I could hear the chants coming from the flat below. It would echo between the buildings for all to hear at 6 am every bloody morning!

My brother Brand always said, "There is no such thing as too much noise, just noise when you don't want it." He would be getting home any minute now; he works nights in a security job at Gunwharf Quays in Portsmouth. Brand is a focused man; he knows what he wants and stops at nothing until he gets it. I guess being super focused and driven is a trait that we both share. Similar to me, Brand made a commitment to save some money each month; unfortunately, his job didn't pay enough to allow leftover money for savings.

My brother took on a second job working the doors at local clubs and bars, so a normal day for him consisted of a twelve-hour day shift, followed by a five-hour shift working as a bouncer. Between these crazy hours, he hit the gym each day for a workout too. What a life, eh? I am glad he is back to only working his main job, but now he has been working the graveyard shift for weeks.

We have been living in this flat for an easy six months now, and I have to admit I have been dancing with the devil. One might think that all is okay, but the truth is that my apple has well and truly fallen off the wagon.

I am grasping at straws and wondering who or what is to blame?

My journey on the slippery slope to hell started just before we moved into this place; there was nothing extraordinary that happened and no big event to cause my weakness. I cannot blame it on the voices or a trauma rising in the ranks. I was weak, and I thought I could handle a few shants. A glass of Jack Daniels soon turned into two, then eight, then twelve ...

I had a blast, and my God, it felt nice as the warmth hit my throat and spread around my stomach, rippling across my chest like a warm blanket. That familiar feeling of alcohol surging through my veins was comforting, but I also experienced the effects of the booze. I missed the normality of drinking with my friends, the socialisation and coupling effect of lower inhibition. I was released from my own inner turmoil of a brain that never stops; like a Duracell battery, it goes on and on and on ...

I was soon punished for my sin as I woke the next day feeling like I had been skull fucked; my head was pounding harder than a seventeen-year-old at prom. The room rocked and moved in waves like the sea, and my heart raced like a cocaine-soaked muscle. I felt scared. It only took my mobile phone to beep once, and I nearly dropped down dead with fear. It was a text from Mercedes; oh God, I can't focus enough to reply. It was all too much as my brain searched for answers. I questioned myself: is this a hangover? It couldn't be one, as this feels like I might die!

I froze as I heard movement outside my door. Like a stalker, I hid behind my dressing gown and peeked through the keyhole. Oh, my fucking God, it is someone wanting to come in. 'Not today, buttercup,' I thought in my head.

My stomach felt queasy, and I soon realised that I needed to poop and fast. As I sat on the toilet, praying to the heavens above to save me, I felt guilty. This was all my fault. I drank last night thinking I was Billie Big Balls, and now look at me. I am cowardly hiding in my toilet, praying that no one sees me. I began to experience an extreme case of paranoia and dark thoughts of hysteria, plus my old friends were back with a vengeance – the dark voices.

I spent the weekend locked in my room, fighting demons and battling the unseen. I was out of my mind.

As Monday landed, I was feeling brighter - not as strong as I usually felt, but I wasn't rocking back and forth on my bed, so it was an improvement, nonetheless. I vowed NEVER to drink again: whiskey is the devil, and rum is my nemesis. Gin is not my friend, and Apple Sourz is a temptress sent to seduce me. It took a day or so, but I was soon feeling back to normal. My brush with insanity was hanging over me like a bill that needed paying, gloomy but avoidable. I continued my work and attended development on a Thursday as I did before. I still did my routine exercise, and the feel-good hormones certainly helped me recover.

However, as Friday approached, I could feel this rotten part of me debating the thrill. I believed that I could drink on Friday nights and recover, ready for Monday. I was only consuming alcohol one evening a week. That's nothing - a drop in the ocean compared to before.

If I could find the right balance, then maybe I could drink and not go bonkers the following day? Electrolytes became my next focus, so I started ensuring that I had easy to eat food for the weekends and vitamin C, including a few bottles of Lucozade drink. The part of my brain that made wise and rational decisions was imprisoned, and a new leader had taken over. The new leader convinced me that the soft drink I was mixing my whiskey with could be the culprit for the following day's hell, so the new leader made an executive decision. From now on, I would only drink whiskey straight, no mixer to poison my body. As a sober person, this all sounds like complete and utter horse shit, but as a drinker wanting to drink, it sounds 100% plausible.

My new life consisted of all my healthy routines of exercising and spiritual development but inserted into it was my Friday night binge session. Weekends were full of solace as I nursed my demons, and then I was back to work every Monday like a new shiny coin. To an outsider, it is probably preposterous for a person to bargain with their sanity, but I felt it was worth the risk. So, there you have it, my dirty little secret. I fell off the wagon, and a new path was formed. I honestly felt that I was still in control and that all I needed was the correct balance, as I munched vitamin C tablets and actually ate before I started to drink. Declining the mixer and drinking my whiskey straight were all part of my crazy solution. The most obvious one was to stop drinking altogether, but I wasn't ready for full-time sobriety back then.

It was fun living with Brand. We went together like peas and carrots; if peas were oddballs and carrots were freaks. Both of us siblings had an obsession with the way that tasks were carried out, perfect for cohabitating with one another. I once recall wandering into the cold kitchen in the early hours of the morning to find Brand just staring out of the window onto the street. It must have been around 5 am, and when I questioned him about it, he said he was waiting for a lady to walk by. Apparently, the lady never picks up her dog's mess, so he was keeping watch. Another night late into the morning, I passed him staring at a wall. He was facing the blank white spot, just concentrating intensely. When I asked him what he was doing, he said that he couldn't sleep.

I have acted just as strangely too. Brand has literally walked in on me trying to count the ceiling ripples; I have also moved to the beat of a dripping tap for hours. I can't throw open food into the bin, but Brand cannot keep open food in the fridge, so at times, our quirks clash. We both liked a spotless house and hated dirt, so scrubbing the flat constantly was a joint task. The real similarity was when I found out that Brand also had a light system inside his head; any task that needed doing was the colour red. All finished tasks were turned to the colour green on completion, and too many tasks made him feel sick, just like me.

Together we were a pair of focused and motivated machines who others viewed as oddballs. My brother never minded me talking to spirits in the flat; he did, at times, wear a tinfoil hat to protect his mind from being read by me. Half as a joke and half serious, he never questioned my spirituality, and he believed what I said to be true. However, he never spoke to spirits; he always said I had a bigger flashlight than he did. The flashlight reference was from a Kevin Bacon film about a man who starts having visions and sees the spirit of a dead girl.

As the months rolled by, I settled into my new regime. I was a party girl every Friday night and a lean, keen exercise machine throughout the week. I met more men and had more antics; a spanner was thrown in the works in 2011 when I fell pregnant. I had been told that I could never have kids; polycystic ovaries and low oestrogen would see to that. I had never wanted children either, which I understand is unusual for a female, but it is my truth. I had a possibility of not one or two but THREE fathers. One guy was a pencil dick twat that lived in the flat below me! The second guy was a construction worker who was handsome and had an ass you just wanted to grab. The third guy was a very round man; he was a good friend who helped me out with little jobs around the house. One of these twats gave me Chlamydia, and I only discovered this from a routine test that the sex clinic did because I was pregnant.

That pregnancy was also when I discovered that I have Rhesus negative blood, B negative to be exact. The nurse pricked my finger twice as she thought it must have been an error with the blood test. When I was pregnant, I experienced a feeling of being whole, like I was doing something that I was put here to do. That may sound strange that it felt so right, yet I still decided to book a termination, but my operation was not needed. My low oestrogen, coupled with other things, resulted in a miscarriage. It was not an experience that I enjoyed, obviously, but at least the decision was taken out of my hands.

From that date onwards, I became the most fertile person in the world. I was either pregnant, having a miscarriage or just getting over one. I did try and use condoms, but I refused other contraception as I feared my already big breasts would get bigger, and there was no way I wanted to put on any weight. I had sacrificed the foods I loved and swapped them all for hours of exercise each day; nothing would make me ruin that hard work! It sounds unreasonable to me now, but at the time, my control issues that affected many areas of my life included my body and food intake.

I love sport and adore most activities, but not many people rise at 5 am for a morning swim to follow up with a run before work. During work, I sometimes managed to fit in a lunchtime workout, then after work, an hour-long exercise at home. I would eat a 500-calorie meal and then enjoy a kickboxing session or a game of football. I was averaging six hours of exercise a day to keep my body looking fit and as an outlet for my focus and control issues.

The months went by, and my development was going great, so I felt it was time to leave Paul's development group. I had been training with him for many years, and I was pretty damn good from my point of view.

The men continued to roll into my life the same as drinks continued to fall into my mouth, but only on a Friday. I was managing not to go completely bonkers, although each time I consumed alcohol, the after-effects were getting darker and harder. I remember going out partying one evening with Brand, Leanne, my mate Taff, and his partner. My brother's friend decided to tag along; his name was Steve. I thought it would be funny to tease him by asking if he wanted to see my dragon tattoo. As the girls stood in the kitchen, watching and waiting for Steve's reaction, I pulled my short blue dress up high towards my breasts. This was necessary to unveil my tattoo; starting from my ribs, the dragon curled down my tanned skin and across my stomach to my pelvic bone. Steve did not even flinch as he kept his eyes firmly on my tattoo to offer his approval; the girls chuckled quietly in the kitchen at my shock attack on Steve.

As the evening went by, we all consumed alcohol and partied through the night at Chicago Rock. As we watered our mouths more back at the flat, others slowly passed out or went home. It appeared the only two drinkers still standing were Steve and me. We selected songs on the jukebox while chatting and talking drink-fuelled rubbish. As a filthy smoker, I slammed open my kitchen window to smoke like a naughty schoolgirl, and the late cold air hit my face. I never did know when to stop drinking, so, as I swayed clumsily to flick the ash from my cigarette, that is when it happened. Steve was sitting by the open window smoking too, and he leaned in at the exact time that I leaned out. We kissed.

I had never really fancied Steve, but the kiss was nice, and I was non-judgmental when it came to men anyway. Steve wanted us to take it further and maybe even as far as the bedroom, but I was not willing to sleep with one of my brother's friends! After shooting Steve down, I stumbled to my room. I closed my eyes and passed out.

That weekend, I thought about Steve a few times, between my dark thoughts and torment. He was tall with nice blue eyes; they sparkled like gems the way Irish eyes do. I knew he had a daughter; I think she was a toddler, if I remember correctly? Nothing came of our drunken and foolish kiss. Not yet, anyway …

I love the smell of bacon cooking, my God; it is heaven. Brand's girlfriend must be here making him dinner. Although I am pretty sure she is a vegetarian, so she must proper love him to cook meat. A few weeks have passed by, and I have been plodding along like a buoy at sea, showing up and being present. Mercedes has asked me if I can teach her some spiritual development skills, and my friend Leanne is keen to learn too. It sounds fun. How cool would it be if I could show them how to do it? We would be like the girls from that witch film - The Craft.

While strolling to work, I can hear the leaves rustling loudly and importantly. It is very windy today, and my hair is flying all over the shop. It is at times like this that I wish I could drive; my brother Elijah was an instructor once upon a time. He always said there was no point in me learning, as I would always be over the drinking limit. Very true for back in the day, but now I was Little Miss Sober; I only drank once a week now. 'Hmmmm, maybe I should learn to drive ...,' I thought to myself.

I phoned Mercedes and shared my good news with her and Leanne; I would start teaching them spiritual development each week. I was so excited to spend more time with two of my closest friends. I had known Leanne since secondary school and Mercedes since we were young kids. They liked each other, and I loved them both dearly. The opportunity to share a gift and knowledge with them both filled my heart with joy.

I couldn't wait to get started, and neither could they ...

My friends and I had agreed on Thursday evenings for our little development circle to gather and practice. I remember feeling happy with this decision as I was used to learning spiritual abilities on this day of the week. I felt excited and a little apprehensive; I wasn't worried about my ability to teach and coach them both. As a qualified teacher and coach, I was used to planning sessions for learning outcomes. I tinkered with the question of whether I was knowledgeable enough to support them. I soon swatted any fears away after reminding myself that we were only going to explore the basics.

A few areas I would stay away from for sure were the ones I was not confident with, like Soul Rescuing. Paul used to talk about this in his classes, but I never really felt drawn to working within this segment. I did get to experience it first-hand at a workshop with Paul, held at Wymering Manor in Paulsgrove. A group of around twenty-five people attended the event, and we investigated energies within the historical building. The property was built in 1042 and was owned by King Edward the Confessor. The manor has been proclaimed Hampshire's most haunted house; legends include ghosts such as The Bloody Nun, Reckless Roddy and many more. The walls were cold and vibrated with energy. As my hands glided over the walls, I ushered them to speak to me. With a sense of anticipation and intrigue, the rooms were curious puzzles as we peered through every window and crevasses like detectives looking for DNA. I recall a foul odour in one of the hallways, and after much debate, I decided it must have been a sign from a spirit.

We can sometimes smell a fragrance like a perfume that a loved one once wore, as a reminder that they are nearby us. The same can be said for yucky smells, too. A familiar perfume or aftershave can be evidence enough to stop us in our tracks. Our loved ones are never far away; they send us messages all the time. I assume they get bored of my pleas for help, but it can't be fun for them, having access to my rambling thought train. I will never forget the lady who brought Mars Bar Cakes. Oh my God, it was like a sex party in my mouth; they tasted so delicious.

It was a cloudy day when I accompanied Paul and his group to Wymering Manor. Thank the heavens it wasn't pouring with rain, as that would have made it much spookier. It was a little surreal moving from room to room, feeling for any change in temperature and sensing any clues to discover the home's hidden secrets.

It was after lunch, and Kayleigh nudged me, turning my attention to a set of small wooden chairs in the communal area. I listened intently as Paul spoke to us about Soul Rescuing; I gingerly closed my eyes and followed his voice. After a short, guided meditation, I was somewhere else, and the noise was deafening. A helicopter must have been flying right above my head, and for a brief moment, I was in a field surrounded by military fighters. I found it hard to focus as my eardrums were being pounded with loud bangs and the noise from that damn thing flying above me. Confusion rushed over me; I couldn't even respond when a soldier shouted at me. It felt like twenty minutes had passed since I entered the field, but in reality, it was a few short moments.

Oh, good, the quiet had returned, and I was safely back in my chair. I opened my eyes and scanned the room. There were people standing on the sidelines who observed us and were unaffected, but I, for one, felt strange. In the distance, I swear I could still hear that metal bird floating above me. I told myself to snap out of it. Paul continued to talk about Soul Rescuing, and comfort was shared when we all heard the helicopter overhead. Slightly out of it and a little bewildered, I attempted to take in all of Paul's words. I caught the part about helping souls to cross over who were unaware that they had died. I have never tried my hand at that task again, and I doubt that I ever will.

It was 6.30 pm, and the girls would be arriving at my flat soon. I did a quick scan, searching for any of my long hairs that may be stranded on the wood flooring, before opting for a few squirts of air freshener on the sofa as I wanted everything to be just right.

There was excitement in the air and not just the air freshener I had previously sprayed. As Leanne and Mercedes chose their seats, I explained to them many of the dos and don'ts of spiritualism. With the gentle sound of Reiki music softly playing in the background, I asked the girls to stand up. I stopped the CD that was currently playing and selected an Elvis Presley song on the jukebox. It was embarrassing and liberating to dance and jump around like childish teens without a care in the world. Free.

The wooden floor vibrated as a result of the loud music that was pumping and our combined awesome dance moves. I am sure the tenant on the floor beneath us appreciated this mini dance party, too, NOT! I swung my hips from left to right, and Leanne pointed towards one direction while wiggling her hips to the opposite side. Sexy Mercedes gyrated her body like a porn star as we sang out loud for all to hear. This act of joyful dancing and singing was to break the ice and lift the energy in the room. As my heart thumped in my chest, it reminded me that I am still alive. Yes, I am still here, with a heart that can still beat.

After settling our thoughts, I guided the group in a meditation; we first visualised protection and grounded ourselves. After opening up our chakras and lifting our vibrations, we began. It was so beautiful and natural for each girl to participate. I remember feeling honoured to be part of their journey to discovering the use of their gifts, it was empowering, and I learnt many lessons too.

Over the next few weeks together, we investigated energies and practised aura readings. On one occasion, we used tools such as flowers and crystals, paper and candles. Throughout the lessons and practices,

I was impressed with Leanne and Mercedes; they were excellent students, and spiritualism came naturally to them. Leanne was enchanted by the crystals, but Mercedes did not feel like she connected with the beautiful gems. I love crystals myself; I use them when I am practising spiritual or reiki healing, and I find them fascinating and powerful.

After each meditation, at the start of every session, I would instruct the group to ask for a gift, and afterwards, we would offer guidance and advice based on their gift. This is a process I had done in my own development class many years ago; the expression was always insightful and useful. For example, a gift of an apple could be symbolic of health, diet or learning. The message or guidance we would offer based on a person's gift would come from inspirational expression from one person to another. The aim would be to give one another a token of advice and words of wisdom; the theory is that the messages were influenced by our higher thinking or the spirit world. What I found extraordinary was how the change from student to teacher had altered my experience; I could easily advise each person on whether they had given a correct message. When either Leanne or Mercedes were delivering words of guidance or struggling to communicate what they were receiving, I could see and hear what they were receiving. It was phenomenal; it was like I had backstage passes to their minds when working with spirit. I have to admit this made my job a hell of a lot easier. To be able to guide them, knowing exactly what they were seeing or trying to figure out, was truly magnificent.

As the circle continued to thrive, it wasn't long before a new member was sent our way, a lovely lady named Ali. Many people were asking to join my development circle, but as professional and serious as we were, it was not official. I was only teaching my friends at their own request; I already had a full-time job and many evening studies and projects. Not forgetting my endless exercise regimes that swallowed my free time like a hungry Pac-Man. So, when others asked if they could join my group, I would usually say no, but on the day I met Ali when swimming, my guides from the spirit world had plans of their own.

I usually liked an early morning swim at a local pool in Portsmouth town; it was nearby my place of employment, so it allowed me to sneak in a swim before work. It wasn't often that I would swim during my lunch breaks, but it wasn't unheard of either. I did try and avoid the rushed twelve o'clock swims, as drying my waist-length hair was a nightmare and stressful when my lunch break was only an hour long. You can imagine a female swimming who does not want to ruin her make-up, with a cranked neck and her head held high, purposely trying to avoid any urine-infected splashes to the face. Kicking her legs out furiously while thrashing about like an angry child, secretly praying to God that the bikini top doesn't come off. And there you have it, my friend; that is exactly what I look like swimming. I detest the chlorinated water that dries out my skin and irritates my flaky scalp like a motherfucker. But you cannot refuse the allure of an all-body workout that tones the body, making a person feel and look fit.

As I swam that day, I spotted Ali in the water. A voice in my head said that she was going to talk to me, and she did. It was inside the changing room that she offered me advice on my flawed technique, suggesting that I should keep my legs straight when thrashing them all over the pool. The conversation continued, and Ali mentioned that she had been told she would emigrate to Australia, and I instantly knew that it was a clairvoyant who had said it. I also knew that I would know the clairvoyant who she had spoken with, which I did. That same voice from earlier suggested that I should invite this stranger Ali to join my group, so I did. Ali was a lovely girl; she was studying Indian Head Massage and worked as an NVQ (National Vocational Qualification) assessor. I believe her parents lived in Spain, where they managed a spiritual retreat. Ali was quiet, but she was more spiritually developed than she let on to most people.

Life was ticking along nicely; I was living my best life, really. I had the men, the money, a good career, my studies and my Friday nights out-out. In the background was the twat from the flat below; we were off and on more times than a northerner's kettle. His mood swings gave me whiplash, with no compensation payout!

My development group was on fire. The girls were performing at a level consistent with people who had been studying mediumistic practices for years. They had come along so fast; I believe this was partially due to me being a qualified and experienced teacher. The other imposing factor was the combined manifestation that we incorporated into every development class. I frequently informed the group of my predicted time frames for their skills to improve; we also used manifestation techniques each week, which set the group running.

I felt it was time to invite strangers to receive readings from the group, this service was free of charge, but they could offer a donation if they wanted to. I recorded all interactions that were allowed by permission, and at the end of each reading, we would listen back and analyse the girl's language and delivery techniques. This was vital to teaching the group the knock-on effects of the language they use when delivering any messages to a sitter from the spirit world. It was also a wonderful opportunity for them to relive the words they had chosen and compare them to what they had seen or heard.

It was during one of their readings to a stranger that I invited a fourth lady to join our group. I was the clairvoyant delivering messages to a beautiful woman named Layla. As soon as she walked into the room, I knew I was the one who would be giving her messages from the spirit world and not one of my students. I could feel something very familiar with this lady, and it didn't take long for me to figure out why. I believe that every person is suited to a certain medium. This is why you can experience a reading from a clairvoyant and feel they were not very good, yet another person could say that they felt the same medium was the best they had ever seen. My theory is that we have a better connection and experience with a sitter based on our previous life experiences. This goes back to when I previously spoke about many practising mediums being older; they require life experience and knowledge to gain the correct skills to deliver delicate messages and navigate choppy waters. It makes sense to me that a medium who has had a deprived childhood may be better suited to deliver messages or healing to a sitter who has experienced similarities within their life. Assuming this is, the medium or clairvoyant has already overcome or healed any similar issues or life barriers.

The beautiful, strong-looking female sitting in front of me had jet black hair and tanned skin; she also looked back at me with these old soul eyes. I could feel her pain crashing into me like a lorry: hard and dangerous. Looking back now, I can analyse just how sensitive her situation was and the dramatic path her life could have taken if I had said the wrong words. Aside from the usual evidence and facts that came through from the spirit world, it was obvious to me that this lady was distraught and struggling mentally with her supernatural abilities. I knew that I couldn't just blurt out the words, but I wanted to say, "You are not crazy, you are psychic, and you have a gift!"

From my own experiences, I understood what a turmoil she was in, thinking she was losing her mind and needed help. I wanted to hold her close and calm her mind. It was not my place to tell her that she wasn't crazy, just like the spirit world never once told me. No matter how many times I sat in the temple of spiritualism praying for an answer, screaming in my head for my guides to inform me whether I was mentally ill or not! I understand the importance of the journey and my path to self-discovery, which I would never have experienced if the guides and spirit world had answered my prayers. It was with this in mind that I chose my language very carefully, not wanting to influence but offering options with no coercion. I laid down the option for Layla to join my development group, which she said yes to in a heartbeat.

My spiritual development group was now a circle of five, Layla, Mercedes, Leanne, Ali and me. Together we would experience a journey to self-discovery that would shape us as human beings forever..................

Chapter 13

My phone vibrates, and I read a text message – *Hey, how are you, hun? How is the great-nephew?*

It was from Steve; I still think about that night we kissed ... We talk via text message and social media, but nothing too X-rated!

I woke up feeling great. Yesterday I experienced the most wonderful day with my girls. We planned a trip to the Isle of Wight to check out an abbey of all places. After an early morning rise, we travelled across the sea on the car ferry with discounted tickets, thanks to Mercedes' dad. The smell of salt in the air combined with our excitement was intoxicating, we felt drunk as skunks, but we were, in fact, sober as a judge.

I felt light being away from Portsmouth, gazing across the short water crossing between Fishbourne and Southsea. I was free.

The weather was sunny at first; my skin warmed as the sunshine kissed my face. All of the girls were looking fine; Layla wore a bright pink dress that stood out a mile against the greenery. Leanne had opted for a yellow summer dress that showed off her tanned legs, while Mercedes' long maxi dress was a midnight blue. I enjoyed the feel of my baggy wide trousers; they floated along as I walked. One might say that my outfit was half bohemian and half hippy. Against the trees and surroundings, we stood out like a sore thumb; it was like a low budget rip off of the girls from New York vacationing in the countryside. Giving absolutely no fucks, we strutted ourselves about like we were on the runway or auditioning for the cover of a best-selling magazine.

As the abbey came into view, our whole mood changed, from being excited trespassers to top energy investigators. I remember drinking everything in, from the fragrance of the garden entrance and fruit hanging from the trees. Pears were shining brightly and deliberate, seductive and tempting. A monk approaching us was enough to bring us back to reality, and our behaviour turned into that of an obedient child at Sunday school. The main entrance door to the abbey was heavy and old looking. As we gingerly walked inside, an instant feeling of trespassing came to mind. I felt like a burglar sneaking in on tiptoe, but instead of diamonds and jewels, all I wanted was energy. Leanne made a beeline for the confession area, which I must admit was a smart choice. As I purposely sought to feel any spots of energy, my body started to rock back and forward as I rooted my feet to the floor. Instinct drew my body to the ground as a surge of remorse rushed through me. I didn't think about the purpose of us linking to the energy within the cold room. Slinking and hovering around the room was a strange experience, but we received what we had come for.

The outside of the abbey revealed a pathway to a graveyard in the rear; it was fascinating reading the dates on the headstones. An interest that I still carry out to this day, I like to find the oldest gravestone in any burial site that I visit. Our aim was to tap into the energy within the abbey and to get a good sense of the building. With Leanne and the others being literally moved by the force, we certainly achieved our goal. When we lifted our vibration and tuned into our other senses, the abbey's energy hit us like a tidal wave. I have experienced a feeling of G-force when I connect to the earth's energy or raise my vibration for spiritual work.

It is not uncommon to feel a tingle or rush as the connection runs through you; this can also happen when I'm feeling another person's aura. As we purposely sought out the energy within the abbey, it was strong and radiated towards us. At times a person can appear to look as if they are rocking back and forth, but the truth is they are holding their body still. A strong energy vibration can literally move a person – gently, of course - and it doesn't hurt.

A few hours later and our time had sadly come to an end, so we hopped in the car in search of food. After eating a very naughty bucket of fried chicken, the girls and I made our way to the sandy beach of Ryde. The sun was playing peek-a-boo with us mere humans, making it cold and cloudy for the best part. When the sun did jump out for a moment or two, we could all pretend that we were on holiday in a faraway land. I could literally see the Spinnaker Tower across the sea, yet I was cushioned by white sand instead of uncomfortable stones. Troubles were in a land that seemed like a world away, and we were here, released on early probation to enjoy just one day. Mercedes wasn't a mum, and Leanne didn't have the dishes to do. Layla was free from her daily tasks, and I wasn't an employment coach. Who puts the ass in class? We do, sipping champagne from small plastic Persil balls. I had forgotten to buy plastic cups, but for some reason, I had five plastic detergent balls - genius. Did people stare at us, thinking we were strange, as we frolicked and screamed on the beach? Of course they did, but we didn't care. Leanne drove us to the car ferry while we listened to Pink on the music player, and I knew I would cherish this day forever.

A few days later, I sat thinking deeply. It was surreal when I thought about our spiritual development circle. It felt as if the spirit world was sending us strangers to give a reading to, and each one came with its own unique lesson for the girls. This one Thursday evening, a plain-looking lady entered my flat, she wore bland colours and had short dark hair. She must have been in her fifties, at a guess. The usual practice was for the girls to facilitate the readings while I recorded them on paper or with a cassette player. If my students said anything they shouldn't or used undesirable language, I would cough. This alerted them to rephrase what they had said. It may sound strict, but I was taking no risks with any messages being miscommunicated. She looked nervous, which is not uncommon, yet excited at the same time. I offered her a seat and started to explain what she should expect from us.

A voice in my head said that I should be the person to carry out this reading, so I did. Leanne, Layla and Mercedes sat by quietly and listened intently. I find that when I am giving a reading, I can be a fast talker. I rub my palms together like I am winding up a toy. It is just a habit, I think. I always start with evidence to demonstrate that the spirit I am connecting to is genuine. I then follow with other evidence, and to end the reading, I deliver the message from the spirit. It can be very hard to give a reading; it takes energy and can be massively confusing at times. It is vital to have complete trust with the spirit world and your guides, as any information that is rejected by the sitter can leave doubt in everyone's mind.

As I moved through the reading, the lady sat on my sofa and declined every piece of information that I gave her, but I continued. It didn't seem to matter whether I was talking to her about a childhood ballet class or her horse-riding hobbies, places of significance, or names and dates. No matter what I said, she replied with a flat no. If my self-esteem or confidence had been lacking, then every answer of no could have rattled me to my core. Throughout the reading, I could sense a gentleman in the room; he stood near the doorway, letting me know he was there.

I had reached the end of the reading when I asked my guides if the time was right, and with a feeling to continue, I opened my mouth. As I began to describe this man to the lady, her whole body shifted. I knew she was here for him and him alone. I spoke softly as I understood why she was in pain; the lady looked me straight in the eyes and asked me who he was?

I replied gently, "He is your son. You lost him very early, maybe within a day or so of his life on this earth."

She burst into tears, and relief cloaked her face like a spell had been cast, a secret she had kept to herself for her entire life. Through wipes of her face with a tissue, she explained to us that no other clairvoyant had brought him through before. Offering possible reasons for this, I explained that maybe she wasn't truly ready before.

Over the next fifteen minutes, I sat smiling at this woman as she now repeated the majority of my reading, explaining how it was all correct. This taught a great lesson as every person who visits a clairvoyant is seeking something. Occasionally, this can make them so focused that they can dismiss all other information or evidence. The session was a perfect learning experience for the girls, and each week we encountered various people with new lessons to learn.

Manifestation is a big focus for me; even scientists have tested many athletes for success, comparing results with visualisation techniques. I have practised the law of attraction and daily meditations too. With athletes, they asked them to visualise the task they were planning to perform; this act encourages memory muscles. If you compare Mr X and Miss X for a two hundred metre race, and they both can run at the same speed for the same amount of time - what imposing factor decides who wins? We are forced to look outside the box. How is their attitude, their confidence and last of all, how high is their motivation to win? If we raced two identical toy cars, which were exactly the same but of different colours, then the race would be a draw. With the exact circumstances matching and the toy cars being equal, there are no imposing factors to consider.

Energy is everywhere around you, electricity, wind, plants, animals and minerals. We are energy, and most crystals have energy. Human thoughts are energy, and the thoughts transfer into actions and responses. Our thoughts shape our reality, having an effect on our life. I believe that our thoughts are living energy that not only affects us as humans but also manifests our reality on this earth plane.

Many of us have heard the terminology, 'You are what you think.' If we strip ourselves down, what is the main difference between being successful and unsuccessful? Many people say it is luck, but luck is a word created to explain multiple choices that lead to an outcome. Is Timmy lucky that he was spotted by a scout at a football match, or was it a series of good choices and habits? Timmy decided that he wanted to play football, so he attended practice twice a week. Timmy acted on feedback and improved his performance, spending all his free time playing football and running drills at home. Timmy played his little heart out at his football match, so was it lucky that he was scouted? Or was it a result of good choices and habits?

It is vital that we recognise the importance of our own thoughts and attitudes towards ourselves and the world around us. A child is fascinated by everything; getting lost in a forest is an adventure, and a hug from their mother can cure all boo-boos.

I have kept a vision board in my house for years; I add goals and pictures of my desires and plans. In the present, my vision board is proudly placed on my refrigerator because I sadly open my fridge often, looking for snacks to appear. Each time I glance at my goals, I fantasise, imagining what it will feel like when I achieve a goal or how I will break the news to friends that I have succeeded in a life-long dream. Every time I create these pictures and predicted emotions in my mind, I send out this message to the universe and to myself: I will succeed; I will achieve my dreams.

I incorporated these same techniques into my development group; we mediated and lifted our vibration to a higher level of thinking. Inside our meditation, we would write down all our desires and objectives relating to our spiritual path and growth. One may ask, is this measurable? Well, my girls gave a reading to a friend of mine after studying with me for six months, and the feedback he gave was he assumed they had been developing for over five years.

It is easier to be positive when everything is going well, like a vicious circle for a person with depression. All the small changes that can improve a person's life; can be too unbearable to do when they are feeling low. I recall being in my darkest times and forcing myself to meditate and listen to the CD suggested to me by the doctor. Maybe my obsession with control is what inevitably sustained me to becoming well again? Yet my OCD didn't raise a red flag level until my mental health deteriorated ...

I only ever used manifestation for life goals, never really for matters of the heart. I had resigned myself to being alone forever. That sounds like a sad and lonely place to be, yet it wasn't. I lived a full life with many friends and way too many jobs. I loved living with Brand and teaching my development group, and my exercise regime kept my happy hormones pumped up high. It was a strange set of events that led me to end up kissing Steve again ...

A few months had passed since *the kiss,* back when I teased Steve with my dragon tattoo. It was January, and I was still adjusting to the cold shit weather. After landing back home from Africa, everything seemed a little pants to me. But with tickets to a gig to watch a Guns N' Roses tribute band, the world was beginning to look a little brighter. A customary pre-drinks party at the flat was in full swing, and guess who was standing by the jukebox looking all flush? Steve had just had a big win on the football, some accumulator bet at the local bookies. I was on a high, not because of Steve, hell no, but because I had my girls with me, and it was a Friday night! That means it is party time for me, plus my birthday was just around the corner, so who was I to deny myself a drink or twelve?

If I am honest, the night was crazy. I remember stumbling around the gig and sipping a nice gin. The song Night Train came on, and then .... NOTHING. Oh God, I must have blacked out. This was happening more and more each time I drank, and it did not sit well with me at all.

I woke up the following day in bed wearing pyjama shorts and a red top, and that is not all I woke up with. Greasy, smelly, disgusting chicken balls were scattered all over my bed. I would like to say that I scraped them into the bin, but no, instead, I popped one into my mouth and down the hatch. As I lay in my Chinese-stinky sheets, flashes of the night before entered my head, and it was epic. I still couldn't remember the actual gig, but I could recall the party at mine before we went out and a few very embarrassing pieces of my behaviour at the after-party. Will I ever learn? I am pretty sure I was pretending to ride Steve in front of everyone while wearing my pyjamas! Well, that seals the deal; he will be mine forever now, for who could resist my sexy stained shorts and red top?

I was too ill to comprehend texting Steve, and I was too scared to leave my room for the voices. My anxiety was right on cue; oh, how I love to feel the world is ending the day after I drink. At least I won't die alone. With the voices chomping in my head, I was never alone. Maybe when I am feeling better, I will invite Steve around to watch a box set. I bet he is a Viking in the sack. I think it may be time to knock the drink on the head for good. No more Friday night drinking sessions; I can't cope with the day after. I need to realise that no concoction will protect me from the dark. I need to protect myself by admitting I will always have a problem with alcohol, and the liquor is no friend to me. From this day forward, I will not drink: no whiskey or gin will pass these lips. I have to be strong, for my mind is broken ...

Chapter 14

The wind was blowing a gale outside. As I listened to the rain drumming against my window, I felt still. Heavy movements outside were evidence that Mother Nature was awake, angry, and resentful. I should really drag my sorry butt out of this warm, cosy bed...

Flashes of her face keep invading my mind like a tornado; who is she, and what does she want?

I first met the girl when I was sitting in the rose garden at Southsea; she wore a pretty green dress made from a heavy material. It was a beautiful day and the fragrances tickling my nostrils were intoxicating; it felt like I was dressed in a sea of roses. Being a sunny and gorgeous day, I took off my open-toed shoes to ground myself. As I stood on the grass, it caressed my feet. The only other person visiting the rose garden that day was the little girl. I had no care for anyone watching me, or who might be wondering what I may be doing. As I softly started to breathe, I connected with the earth. Wiggling my toes to feel the dirt beneath me, energy from the earth penetrated through me. Cries of laughter and joy were carried along in the light breeze. The sound of children playing in the sand park next door was faint, but they were audible.

As I tilted my head towards the sky, my skin warmed as the rays of the sun caressed my face. I always feel lifted when I am outside, and a smile crept across me as I pictured many of my walks home. I danced and swayed with the trees, mimicking their every movement. Along the busy main roads, cars and passers-by stopped to stare, probably wondering what the hell I was doing! That sums me up rather nicely: the weird girl who talks to thin air and dances with the trees. It is not my intention to make others feel uncomfortable, but I am too free to worry about my impact on others. What will people think of me if I dance with the trees? These are not questions that enter my mind or are considered serious thoughts. I am me; I do what feels right, and at this very moment, I want to sing to the sky.

As I stood in the rose garden singing my soul to the sky above, a voice joined me. This beautiful little creature was singing with me, and with my interest piqued, I slowly opened my eyes and turned towards the sound. A short human was stood nearby, with red hair that hung in locks down to her waist. At first, I believed she must have been a runaway, who had some scared parent running around the sand park, screaming her name, but I couldn't hear any cries of a desperate parent. She said her name was Sadie and that her doll was called Gemma, but she preferred it when others called her Gemzies. My eyes couldn't really focus well due to the unusually bright day we were having for springtime. I was not too happy having my moment of peace interrupted by this child, but she did sing along with me only moments ago.

It felt dangerous to be here alone with this young girl. What if the police came storming into the garden thinking I had kidnapped her? I decided to help her find her parents, but each time I asked where they were, she just replied sadly with the fact they were not here. Desperate and worried, I scanned the entrance and exit for any signs of petrified adults, but without any luck. As I turned back towards the girl, she was gone. She had vanished into thin air, quicker than my payday money does. The rose garden is a large area, with grass in the centre and rose bushes surrounding the borders. It was impossible for her to have exited the garden without me witnessing it, not a chance in hell. I had assumed she was a spirit child, not living on this earth plane anymore.

A few days later, I returned to the exact same place with my girls from my development group. It was exciting to be there, armed with a box of eggs, for a manifestation session. Layla was enjoying the outside and pure beauty of the garden, while Leanne was giggling like a schoolgirl. She kept joking about us egging some houses; obviously, we would never do that, but the joke tickled Leanne to her core. I instructed the girls to open up their chakras, connect with the earth, and then walk the perimeter seeking an individual spot for the next part of the session.

As silent as a cloud rolling on by, I watched as Sadie, the little red-haired girl, followed Leanne around the garden. Jumping from one foot to another, she looked happy and playful. I felt privileged to be a witness to such joy, to be able to see what most others cannot. What an honour, what a beautiful thing. My thoughts were soon snapped away as I realised we had come to the garden for a purpose; we cracked up our offering to the earth. We watched as raw eggs smoothly poured into the dirt and stones. It was a magical evening, like most of our nights spent together. Or at least it was until Mercedes suggested a night on the town to celebrate our development coming to an end.

My mind twisted and turned at the prospect of a night out on the tiles. My mouth watered as I thought of the gin, whiskey, and all the other delicious wet demons in bottles. I had vowed never to drink again; I must stick to my word - this shouldn't even be a debate!

A decision had been made. We were going out to celebrate, and why shouldn't we; don't we deserve a few hours of fun?

As I pulled on my dress and splashed my neck and wrists with Coco Chanel Mademoiselle, it was official; we were going out. I had set myself a three drink limit; as an alcoholic, that was as good as not drinking. For every alcoholic drink that I ordered, I planned to down at least three soft drinks as spacers' in-between. We danced the night away in heels that were way too high for my liking. Leanne shook her booty like her life depended on it, and Mercedes was grinding like a stripper dancing for cash. It was a perfect night, and I was completely and utterly sober! Yes, I had consumed three alcoholic beverages, but I sipped them like a tiny bird perched on a fountain. As I took off my clothes and climbed into my cold bed, I let my thoughts turn to Steve ...

As I woke the next day, I checked my mind. How was I feeling? Was I okay? Were the dark thoughts lurking around the corner? My body wasn't shaking, and my heart seemed to beat to its sober rhythm. My final slip of drinking three drinks had paid off. I felt a little guilty, though, like I was a fraud. No, Bryony, push any dark thoughts aside as they can only lead to bad things ... The darkness washed over me like a blanket of silk, delicate and smooth.

Okay, so I am sitting in my room, wondering about all my decisions and how they got me to where I am today. Am I happy, or am I in denial? I decide to start researching the subject on Google because, come on, if Google doesn't know, then no one will, or at least that's the day and age that we now live in.

My room is quiet. I can hear the music from my neighbour downstairs, who obviously thinks that no one else can afford a radio or electricity, so they blast their tunes out for all to hear 24/7.

I look around at all my stuff. Stuff, stuff, stuff everywhere, all this stuff I feel I need to be happy and get by in life. All the essentials like Coco Chanel No.5, Angel and Viktor Rolfe at £80.00 a bottle, my widescreen TV that sits staring at me like it is going to shout, "Come on, your eyes can't be so bad that you need a 50-inch screen."

I look around and feel the need to know why people are so lost, unhappy and ill. I meditate, which is something I have done ever since I fell victim to stress, drugs and alcohol. I shudder at the thought of how I lived my life, an emptiness only an addict can know. Not feeling enough and at the same time feeling so much that it bears down on your soul, like a weight several times heavier than you that will always win. Like a dark tunnel of waking up in strange places, with people who are not the church-going type, but the ones who will steal your washing or nick your car when you are out. I push the thoughts to the dark place in my mind, with all the other secrets of sex, lies, and violence. I am trying to be positive: think about how far you have come and the stories you can tell and will. I take a deep breath. We all have a soul; some are good, and some are bad, but has yours ever been empty?

Positive Bryony: Come on, be brave. I begin to listen to the gentle music of Buddhism as I first open my mind and quieten it down. I then pack away all the bad things that happened that day, a trick I learned in therapy when I was a child. I lift my vibration and ask my guides for advice.

"Am I on the right path? Should I be working where I do? Am I a good person? Will I ever find peace or feel contentment? Please give me the information I need."

I clear my mind, and I see ticks like if you got a question correct on a test, I confirm this is for my job and career as a teacher. I then ask where my destiny lies, and I see water as in an ocean plus the month of March. Could this be connected to the dolphins I always see when I meditate?

I question my trust and doubt whether I am crazy, which I have done on many occasions. However, even Portsmouth's finest doctors assure me that I am sane, and they have no reason to section me. Plus, the people I have helped, the things I know, I have proven beyond a doubt that the gift I have is true ... or have I?

I begin my normal practice of bargaining.

"Please tell me or show me what I am here to do, and I will do it. I will sacrifice my own happiness for this. I will not pursue a man or any goals except to serve my purpose, please just guide me, and I will do it. What shall I do?"

My hand starts frantically writing a song on some paper. It feels like I have no control, the words just flow, and I read them back and wonder what this message could mean. I then start to draw a cross that turns into a tree. I start writing things all over the picture, food, shelter, warmth, protection; soon, I have at least ten words. I look to the side of the drawing and write TO SOME IT IS JUST A TREE. Then one of the words catches my eye as it reads 'paper.' I can feel my brain making the connection as I am still tuned into my inspirational writing from the spirit world. Paper, books, words, others' points of view, people, connected, trees, roots, basic needs, happiness. Then it hit me: what makes people happy, and what is it?

I now know what I must do. I have to find this answer and share it with everyone in the form of a book!

I feel elevated, unlike my miserable self an hour ago, when I had decidedly given up on my own happiness and was willing to give it all up. To complete my purpose and focus on that burning question, now I have purpose.

"Thank you," I whisper aloud.

The next part of my journey has been revealed to me, and I WILL NOT FAIL! ...

About the Author

Bryony Best was born and raised in Portsmouth, United Kingdom. She is currently residing in Hayling Island with her fiancé and her much loved Chihuahua dog named Luna.

Bryony works as a Holistic Therapist and lives a happy life of mindfulness and wellbeing.

Bryony drew on experiences from her life to write this book, and her inspiration to share her story with the world is to shine a light on mental health, addiction and trauma.

Bryony has trained and studied Spiritualism for many years and still practices and teaches groups to this day. Bryony is a Reiki Master with qualifications for Crystal Healing. By combining these practices with Spiritual Healing, Bryony has found balance within her mind.

The Girl from Pompey – Conversations with the Dead is the prequel to Bryony's first publication (The Girl from Pompey – Discovering the Key to Happiness and Fulfillment).

Bryony Best

Final Message to the Reader

I would like to thank you from the bottom of my heart for purchasing and reading this book. Please do consider reading my first book, which this book is a prequel to - The Girl from Pompey – Discovering the Key to Happiness and Fulfilment.

I hope this book has touched you on a deeper level or given you some hope if hope is needed.

I do ask that you please take the time to leave a review on the site where you purchased this book, and do also add your review to Goodreads - if you have an account with them.

Please upload a picture with your review to your Social Media platforms; this will help others to find my book.

Website - www.bryonybest.com

Twitter - @bryony_best

Instagram - @bestbryony

Facebook – The Girl from Pompey

TikTok - @bryonybest

"Never hide your magic; let your light shine so bright that your friends will need sunglasses."

Bryony Best

Printed in Great Britain
by Amazon